SHARING THE PEN

INTERACTIVE WRITING WITH YOUNG CHILDREN

Gail E. Tompkins

California State University, Fresno

Stephanie Collom

Fresno Unified School District, Fresno, California

PEARSON

Merrill
Prentice Hall

Upper Saddle River, New Jersey
Columbus, Ohio

Library of Congress Cataloging-in-Publication Data

Tompkins, Gail E.
    Sharing the pen : interactive writing with young children/Gail E. Tompkins, Stephanie Collom. p. cm.
    Includes bibliography references.
    ISBN 0-13-112965-1
    1. English language–Composition and exercises–Study and teaching (Early childhood)
    2. Language arts (Early childhood) I. Collom, Stephanie. II. Title.

    LB1139.5.L35T66 2004
    372.62'3–dc21

                         2003042952

Vice President and Executive Publisher: Jeffery W. Johnston
Senior Editor: Linda Ashe Montgomery
Editorial Assistant: Laura Weaver
Production Editor: Mary M. Irvin
Design Coordinator: Diane C. Lorenzo
Cover Designer: Ali Mohrman
Cover Art: Austin Lorenzo, age 6
Production Manager: Pam Bennett
Director of Marketing: Ann Castel Davis
Marketing Manager: Darcy Betts Prybella
Marketing Coordinator: Tyra Poole

This book was set in Novarese medium by Carlisle Communications, Ltd. It was printed and bound by Phoenix Color Corp. The cover was printed by Phoenix Color Corp.

Pearson Prentice Hall™ is a trademark of Pearson Education, Inc.
Pearson® is a registered trademark of Pearson plc
Prentice Hall® is a registered trademark of Pearson Education, Inc.
Merrill® is a registered trademark of Pearson Education, Inc.

Pearson Education Ltd.
Pearson Education Singapore Pte. Ltd.
Pearson Education Canada, Ltd.
Pearson Education—Japan

Pearson Education Australia Pty. Limited
Pearson Education North Asia Ltd.
Pearson Educación de Mexico, S.A. de C.V.
Pearson Education Malaysia Pte. Ltd.

10 9 8 7 6 5 4 3 2 1
ISBN: 0-13-112965-1

PREFACE

SHARING THE PEN: INTERACTIVE WRITING WITH YOUNG CHILDREN

A few years ago, I had the pleasure of attending an institute sponsored by the San Joaquin Valley Writing Project in Fresno, California. I did a presentation on interactive writing, an exciting writing strategy I had just begun using with my kindergarten class. A few months later, Dr. Gail Tompkins asked me to coordinate a weeklong series of workshops on interactive writing in a nearby school district. As I started contacting teachers and viewing their presentations on interactive writing, I began to realize even more what a powerful teaching strategy interactive writing is and appreciate the variety of ways teachers were integrating interactive writing into their daily writing activities.

The success of the workshops led Dr. Tompkins to the idea of putting all the different ways teachers were using interactive writing into a resource book that we could share with other teachers. We started meeting with Teacher Consultants in the Writing Project, discussing how we were using interactive writing in our classrooms. Soon, each of the teachers started writing about his or her favorite and most successful interactive writing lessons. We met over a series of months, reading each other's chapters and sharing thoughts and insights. We collected and analyzed students' work samples and tried out each other's lessons, which led to more discussion and refinement of our lessons and chapters.

THE RESULT

What resulted from the many exciting months of collecting, refining, and experimenting is the book in your hands. We hope this text will not only help you to understand interactive writing, but will provide you with many classroom-tested, meaningful ways of implementing interactive writing in your classroom.

Interactive writing is the bridge between more teacher-directed (or modeled) writing and independent writing. We made two important discoveries in looking so closely at interactive writing:

1. Teachers can easily differentiate instruction to meet the needs of any student during an interactive writing session.
2. Phonemic awareness, concepts about print, phonics, and vocabulary development can be incorporated easily into each interactive writing lesson.

We have many students in the San Joaquin Valley who speak English as a second language, as well as many struggling readers and writers; consequently, these discoveries were very important to us.

Because interactive writing is a strategy most commonly used with emergent and early writers, many chapters in this text are most applicable to kindergarten through third grade. We have, however, included a chapter on using interactive writing with older, struggling students.

Early chapters focus on the theory and implementation of interactive writing. The balance are individual lessons, or series of lessons, that teachers can use immediately in their own classrooms.

The San Joaquin Valley Writing Project is part of the National Writing Project (NWP), and there are NWP sites in every state. If you are interested in learning more about the NWP or joining your local site, contact the National Writing Project through its website at http://www.writingproject.org.

CONTENTS

AN INTRODUCTION TO INTERACTIVE WRITING

Linda Boroski

In recent years, increasing numbers of teachers have been learning about and implementing a form of shared writing known as interactive writing. The more teachers use this strategy, the more they discover its power for teaching key literacy concepts to young writers, nonwriters, and writers of diverse language backgrounds. Through the use of this instructional strategy, teachers have found a way to reach students for whom the concept of writing or the ability to write has not yet been developed.

What is interactive writing? How does it work? And why is this teaching strategy so effective for such a wide range of students who are learning to write? The purpose of this introduction is to answer these questions so that teachers using this book can begin to incorporate interactive writing into their instructional repertoire and experience firsthand the benefits of interactive writing for students. The subsequent chapters give specific examples of interactive writing lessons that teachers have successfully used in their classrooms.

WHAT IS INTERACTIVE WRITING?

Interactive writing is a form of shared writing in which the teacher and a group of students work together to write a text. Interactive writing stems from the language experience approach developed by Ashton-Warner (1963) in which students, after being involved in an experience, dictate sentences about the experience while the teacher records the sentences on a chart. Much like the language experience approach, interactive writing, a process developed by McKenzie (1985), is predicated on the notion that children will learn to read and write text more readily if they themselves are the authors of this text, and if the text is based on familiar topics or experiences. The critical difference between the two instructional strategies is that with the language experience approach, the teacher acts as scribe, whereas with interactive writing, the children share the pen with the teacher to write the words on the chart. With this turning over of the pen to the children, they become actively involved not only in reading, but also in learning conventions of writing, concepts about print, and spelling patterns.

HOW DOES INTERACTIVE WRITING WORK?

Interactive writing follows a series of steps that repeat in a cycle as the text is created. The following six steps form a basic outline and rationale for the interactive writing cycle. In addition to following the steps, the teacher will need to gather these

1

materials: chart paper, felt-tip marking pens in a variety of colors, and correction tape. It is also important to have a meaningful topic about which to write and a skill or strategy focus in mind, based on student need; literature studies, theme cycles, studies in the content areas, field trips, or other shared experiences can all serve as meaningful and authentic writing topics. Once the teacher has gathered the necessary materials and has chosen the topic, the steps described here are followed.

STEPS IN INTERACTIVE WRITING

Step 1: Negotiate a Sentence. The teacher and students collaborate to write a meaningful text that students can read. According to McCarrier, Pinnell, and Fountas (2000), "interactive writing is based on oral language" (p. 11). The text can focus on a wide variety of topics and can take a variety of forms such as lists, survey questions, innovations on stories or poems, invitations, letters, recipes, and daily news. During the writing of the text, many skills can be developed, including letter formation, punctuation, capitalization, word boundaries, directionality, affixes, phonetic structures, vocabulary development, and spelling. The teacher has an active role in negotiating the text, another difference from the language experience approach in which the teacher takes direct dictation from the students. By playing this active role, the teacher can incorporate the teaching of skills and writing conventions into the interactive writing lesson. For example, if the students are ready to learn about the use of commas in a series, the teacher can design a lesson in which the class creates a sentence that has a list of things in it. The teacher can also serve as a model for English language learners, modeling correct English grammar and sentence structure.

Step 2: Count the Words on Fingers. The teacher pronounces the agreed-upon sentence slowly, and holds up one finger for each word spoken. The process is repeated with both teacher and students counting the words on fingers while slowly saying the sentence. Counting words on fingers clarifies the concept that a sentence is composed of words. It also makes clear, both visually and physically, that there is a space between both fingers and words. If the teacher is careful to hold up fingers so that students see the progression from left to right, then the directionality of print is also reinforced.

Step 3: Recall the Word to Be Written and Stretch the Word. The first word to be written now becomes the focus. The teacher articulates the word slowly, using a technique known as "stretching the word." As the word is stretched, or spoken slowly, the students listen for the individual phonemes that make up the word. This word stretching can take a variety of forms depending on the preference of the teacher: Some teachers stretch their hands apart slowly as they say the word; others stretch a rubber band; still other teachers pull the word out of their mouths slowly. Regardless of how the word is stretched, the important aspect of slowly articulating the word so that children attend to the individual sounds in the word remains unchanged. As children attend to the sounds in words, their phonemic awareness, or ability to hear sounds in words, is enhanced, and the process of encoding words using alphabet letters becomes increasingly clear.

Step 4: Share the Pen. A student volunteer uses the pen, usually a felt-tip marking pen, to write part of the word or the whole word on the chart paper. Conventional spelling is used because one of the goals of interactive writing is to write a text that all can read. Therefore, the student scribe will need support, which can come from a number of sources. Sometimes the teacher uses a different colored pen to write a word or portion of a word that the children are unsure of. In addition to the teacher, other students, word walls, word family charts, class name lists, and alphabet charts are valuable means of support for students writing the word.

Inevitably, students will make mistakes while writing a word. To correct errors, teachers place adhesive labels or tape, or even a patch of the chart paper, over the error. The child can correct the error by writing on the patch. It is important during the correction of errors that children are praised for their attempts and supported in their willingness to try, and also reassured that mistakes are commonplace and acceptable.

An interactive writing lesson is an ideal setting for the teacher to make adaptations to the lesson to ensure that the student sharing the pen will have success. Sometimes, teachers will have students in the group write on individual dry-erase boards, small chalkboards, or clipboards as the text is created on the chart; this gives children the opportunity to practice spelling and letter formations before going to the chart, and it also keeps all children engaged throughout the lesson. Teachers provide varying degrees of support to students, depending on their strengths. For example, reminding students that the first word in the sentence begins with a capital letter can eliminate an error.

Step 5: Point and Read. Once the word has been written on the chart, the teacher or a student can use the pointer to point to the word as it is read. The reciprocal nature of reading and writing is emphasized during this step.

Step 6: Recall the Entire Sentence to Be Written, Then Go Back to Step 3. The teacher and students repeat the sentence they have agreed to write to refresh their memory. This helps the students start learning the skill of keeping an entire thought, or sentence, in their heads until they are able to write it down. The next word in the sentence becomes the new focus. The steps to follow during an interactive writing lesson are summarized in Figure 1.

WHY DOES INTERACTIVE WRITING WORK?

The basis for interactive writing stems from two things: the characteristics of emergent writers and the theory of Russian psychologist Lev Vygotsky (1896–1934). Emergent writers notice print in their environment; they recognize familiar words and letters on trucks, food packages, and cards from Grandma. Emergent writers are confident in their knowledge of the alphabet and are able to use those letters in their writing. Their writing includes many conventional features, such as letters and words. These more advanced concepts have emerged from children's earlier understandings about print that they have noticed in their environment.

FIGURE 1 Steps in an interactive writing lesson.

1. *Negotiate a sentence.* The teacher and students collaborate to write a meaningful text that can be read.
2. *Count the words on fingers.* As the teacher repeats the agreed-upon sentence slowly, one finger is held up for each word spoken.
3. *Recall the word to be written and stretch the word.* The teacher articulates the word slowly using a technique known as "stretching the word." As the word is stretched, or spoken slowly, the students listen for the individual phonemes that make up the word.
4. *Share the pen.* A student volunteer uses the pen to write part of the word or the whole word on the chart paper. Conventional spelling is used.
5. *Point and read.* Once the word has been written on the chart, the teacher or a student can use the pointer to point to the word as it is read.
6. *Recall the entire sentence to be written, then go back to step 3.* The teacher and students repeat the sentence they have agreed to write to refresh their memory. The next word in the sentence becomes the new focus.

Emergent writers are engaged in their writing efforts. They are working hard to understand how written language works, how to encode the sounds of their language with alphabet letters, while building a writing vocabulary of high-frequency words such as *the* and *was*. They know that their writing does not look like adults' writing, but they are willing to devote large amounts of time and effort to even small writing tasks.

At this time in the emergent writer's life, the child is in what Vygotsky (1978) termed the "zone of proximal development" for writing tasks. This zone of proximal development is the range of activities that the child cannot yet perform alone, but can perform successfully with guidance from others who are more knowledgeable. During interactive writing, the teacher provides guidance to the children during the lesson so that they can successfully write text that adheres to all of the conventions of print.

During interactive writing, teachers scaffold the children's writing efforts. Scaffolding is another idea of Vygotsky's; it refers to a teacher, adult, or other competent person supporting the efforts of a child who is performing a task in the zone of proximal development. As the teacher works with children to negotiate a sentence, counts words with children on fingers, stretches words slowly, and assists children in writing, the teacher is scaffolding the writing efforts of emergent writers.

Interactive writing works with children whose writing ability is emerging because they are in need of the scaffolding support of a more knowledgeable person. The interactive writing lesson is constructed to provide exactly this support so that the child can perform the writing task that is too difficult or complex to perform independently.

CONCLUSION

"Interactive writing is not simply a mechanical process to be followed in order to produce a text. While the product is important, the process is what has most value" (McCarrier, Pinnell, & Fountas, 2002, p. 9). Now that you know what interactive writing is, as well as how and why it works, you are ready to read the exciting chapters that make up this book. These chapters are full of wonderful ideas for lessons that teachers have developed for use in their own classrooms. If you are interested in learning how to use interactive writing in conjunction with English language development, in the writing process, in research writing, or in any number of other areas, read on!

REFERENCES

Ashton-Warner, S. (1963). *Teacher*, New York: Simon & Shuster.

McCarrier, A., Pinnell, G., & Fountas, I. (2000). *Interactive writing: How language & literacy come together, K–2*. Portsmouth, NH: Heinemann.

McKenzie, M. G. (1985). Shared writing: Apprenticeship in writing. *Language Matters*, 1–5.

Vygotsky, L. S. (1978). *Mind in society: The development of higher psychological processes*. Cambridge, MA: Harvard University Press.

THE WRITING CONTINUUM: LEVELS OF TEACHER SUPPORT

Stephanie Collom

Our students come to school at varying levels of writing proficiency. As teachers, we need to demonstrate for our students how to write and what steps writers must go through to communicate their ideas to others. According to Routman (1991, p. 161), "Our students must have writing models if they are to become writers, and we teachers need to be those models." Teachers must understand that there are levels of teacher support that we need to provide to our students to enable them to become proficient writers. The level of teacher support is based on student need; even more proficient writers may still need to participate in modeled and shared writing activities if the strategies or skills are new to them. The levels begin with modeled writing, where the teacher does all of the writing, and proceed to independent writing, where the student does all of the writing and very little teacher support is needed. Interactive writing is the bridge to independence—according to Vygotsky (1978, p. 87), "what a child can do with assistance today she will be able to do by herself tomorrow." The students begin to work in their "zone of proximal development," doing more work independently, but with the teacher there to scaffold their thought processes and help them with the unknown. This chapter explains the different levels of teacher support and gives ideas for activities to help the teacher scaffold student learning.

LEVEL 1: MODELED WRITING

We learn to do many of the things in our lives by watching others; after we see others perform the tasks, we try them ourselves. This also applies to writing. Many children arrive at school having seen little writing demonstrated by others at home. Many children have never discussed writing with their parents or peers and have not experimented with writing, or if they have, they may not have shared the writing with others. Students may become frustrated and may not be willing to take risks with their writing if they have no clear idea about how to get started, how to organize their ideas, or how to revise and edit. Teacher modeling of writing process activities is crucial for students at all developmental levels. Patricia Cunningham and Richard Allington (1994) describe teacher modeling as "writing and talking about what they [the teachers] are thinking as they are writing" (p. 101).

According to Cunningham and Allington, teachers should model some part of the writing process every day. Younger children could be gathered on the floor in front of a white board, chalkboard, easel, or overhead projector. It is important that teachers articulate all of their thinking processes so they are clear to the students. This shows students what teachers are thinking and how they are organizing their thoughts. They may talk about possible subjects or demonstrate clustering. The topics are teacher generated—the teacher does all the thinking and writing, and the students are observers of the process. The teacher then starts writing, speaking slowly, pausing to think about what to write next, thinking aloud about the spellings of difficult words, looking around the room and demonstrating where to go when students need help with a spelling (e.g., word walls, student dictionaries, environmental print), trying out different words in a sentence to find which one sounds the best, deciding on punctuation, and rereading the written text to see how it sounds when read aloud. The teacher is modeling and thinking aloud all of his or her own thought processes and organizational skills while writing. Seeing the teacher go through the process helps the students to understand the kinds of things they can write about, how to organize their ideas, and where to go when help is needed. When the teacher, through observation of students' writing, sees a skill (such as punctuation, capitalization, tense, spelling, prewriting, revising, and editing) that needs to be demonstrated for the students, he or she can integrate the skill into modeled writing lessons.

LEVEL 2: SHARED WRITING

In shared writing, "the teacher's role is an enabling, supportive one that encourages and invites students to participate and enjoy writing experiences they might not be able to do on their own" (Routman, 1991, p.60). Cunningham and Allington (1994, p. 90) describe shared writing as "a process in which the teacher and children write together." The advantage of shared writing is that it can be used with students of all ages and developmental levels. The teacher can act as a scribe and write exactly what the students dictate, or the teacher and students can jointly negotiate a text, and the teacher writes what is agreed upon by the group. Because it is usually done in an informal setting, all students feel comfortable contributing and concentrate on composing.

The Language Experience Approach (LEA), one type of shared writing, can be used with individual children or with small groups. The teacher writes down exactly what the student dictates, whether it is grammatically correct or not. The purpose is for the student to see that writing is speech written down; if a student says, "My tooth got broke" but the teacher writes "My tooth fell out," the student may still read it as "My tooth got broke." If the teacher is trying to demonstrate that what is said can be written down and read, then the child's exact words should be used.

When working with the whole class, or a small group where everyone has something to contribute to the text, the text can be negotiated between the teacher and the students. The teacher can in this case "negotiate" standard written English. Standard usage should be emphasized in this type of shared writing because the text may be used as a chart or book in the room that all the students refer to as a resource for later reading and writing. The teacher can listen to all the ideas and suggestions, and then orally negotiate the ideas with the students until a consensus is reached on what will be written down. The teacher then models the process of writing down what has been agreed upon, demonstrating for the students the connection between oral and written language, as well as the conventions of writing. The text can also be used to model revision and editing.

LEVEL 3: INTERACTIVE WRITING

An extension of shared writing is interactive writing. As with shared writing, the teacher and students negotiate the text, but instead of the teacher acting as scribe, the teacher and students "share the pen"—the students write what they can and the teacher fills in the rest. Interactive writing also differs from shared writing in that more attention is paid to the sounds within the individual words and to spelling patterns (Fountas & Pinnell, 1996). Unlike shared writing, this approach is used almost exclusively with kindergarten and first-grade writers. After the text is negotiated, the teacher and students say each word slowly, listening for the sounds within the word. The students then share the pen with the teacher, writing the letters or clusters of letters that stand for the sounds they hear. The teacher may have the students refer to prompts, such as a picture alphabet chart, to help them make the sound-symbol connection. The teacher fills in the letters that the students have not yet learned. The sentence is reread after each word is written, and then the process is repeated with the next word of the text. As the teacher and students work together on the text, the teacher can focus on conventions such as concepts about print, spelling, capitalization, punctuation, and letter formation.

LEVEL 4: GUIDED WRITING

In guided writing, students write with teacher supervision and guidance to complete a writing assignment. Usually the assignment is structured, and students have the opportunity to practice writing strategies and skills (Tompkins, 2003). Guided writing, like guided reading, is usually done in small groups so that the teacher can observe and assist each child. Based on student need, the teacher models a form or structure during a minilesson for the whole class or a small group, brainstorms possible ideas with students, and works with students to write collaborative pieces. The students then use the same form to write their own piece (Tompkins, 2003). For example, the teacher could model some form of poetry, such as: "I wish . . . ," "If I were . . . ," color, pattern, or five-senses poems (Tompkins, 2004; Tompkins & McGee, 1993). The students would brainstorm possible writing ideas, write a poem collaboratively with the teacher's support, and then write a poem on their own using the same formula and the brainstorming chart for ideas. They are guided by the teacher in such a way as to foster independence, but at the same time guaranteeing success because of the level of teacher and peer support.

LEVEL 5: INDEPENDENT WRITING

Independent writing is the level with the most student independence and least teacher control and support. Students participate in process writing, writer's workshop, and writing groups. They self-select their topics or extend a guided writing idea and go through the process writing stages on their own—prewriting, drafting, revising, editing, publishing—asking the assistance of the teacher or peers when they feel it's necessary. They work at their own pace on the pieces they want to work on, participating in writing groups to receive feedback and help from their peers. Some of the work they may publish and share with others, and some of the writing may be personal, such as a journal or log. After students have had experience with modeled, shared, interactive, and guided writing, they are prepared for the challenges of working on their own and know where to go when they need assistance.

Activities across the continuum don't progress linearly from modeled to independent, but may progress from modeled to shared to interactive writing, then may go back to shared writing, then may go to guided writing, then back again to modeled writing activities. The kinds of activities chosen depend on the level of teacher support the students need to acquire the skills and strategies that will make them successful writers. Figure 2 shows the levels of teacher support across the continuum, the purpose of each level, the roles of the teacher and students, and

TEACHER CONTROL ⟵————————————⟶ STUDENT CONTROL

	MODELED ⟷ WRITING	SHARED ⟷ WRITING	INTERACTIVE ⟷ WRITING	GUIDED ⟷ WRITING	INDEPENDENT WRITING
Teacher and Student Roles	Teacher thinks aloud and writes text.	Students and teacher create text; teacher is scribe.	Teacher and students "share the pen" to write the text.	Teacher provides topic or form; students do the writing.	Students choose topics and do the writing.
Purpose	To demonstrate a writer's thought processes.	To demonstrate that writing is speech written down.	Letter/ sound relationships, conventions of print.	Guided support through minilessons.	Freedom of choice and ideas.
Activities	Whole-class or small-group demonstrations on overhead, chart, or easel.	LEA, personal experiences, field trips, retellings, class books or charts.	Personal experiences, field trips, retellings, class books, or daily news.	Formula poems, frames, ABC books, or collaborative pieces.	Journals, process writing, writer's workshop, or writing groups.

FIGURE 2 Continuum of teacher support for student writers.

activities for each level. When teachers serve as writing models and support students' thought processes by providing activities with teacher support based on students' needs, the students will become independent writers.

REFERENCES

Cunningham, P., & Allington, R. (1994). *Classrooms that work: They can all read and write*. New York: HarperCollins.

Fountas, I., & Pinnell, G. S. (1996). *Guided reading*. Portsmouth, NH: Heinemann.

Routman, R. (1991). *Invitations*. Portsmouth, NH: Heinemann.

Tomkins, G.E. (2003). *Literacy for the 21st century*. (3rd ed.). Upper Saddle River, NJ: Merrill/Prentice Hall.

Tompkins, G.E. (2004). *Teaching writing: Balancing process and product* (4th ed.). Upper Saddle River, NJ: Merrill/Prentice Hall.

Tompkins, G. E., & McGee, L. M. (1993). *Teaching reading with literature: Case studies to action plans*. New York: Merrill/Macmillan.

Vygotsky, L. S. (1978). *Mind in society: The development of higher psychological processes*. Cambridge, MA: Harvard University Press.

GROUPING OPTIONS TO SUPPORT STUDENT SUCCESS

Susan McCloskey

In my classroom, I select the group size most appropriate for the kind of interactive writing experience that is going to take place. Moreover, I don't always use the same grouping techniques for each interactive writing experience. I let the group experience be risk-free communication that provides a means for successful learning. Interactive writing allows my students to participate in the control of their learning; this control, in conjunction with ample support from me, guarantees their success and independence.

During an interactive writing experience, my responsibility as a teacher is to scaffold student learning as I provide direct instruction in areas such as alphabet, conventions of print, concepts about print, content, oral language, reciprocity, and spelling. Because interactive writing requires the teacher to support each child at the child's learning level, it is important to know the students' needs and strengths well.

In this chapter, I define three major grouping options: working with the whole group, working with a small group, and working in a paired situation. In all three grouping options, I use examples or sample experiences that focus on different versions of the story *The Three Little Pigs*.

Grouping is an important consideration when using the interactive writing process. I group students for specific purposes: For each group of students that I work with, I choose one or two teaching points that students have demonstrated a need to learn. Children do not all have the same needs or the same interests. In my classroom, each student's success is increased when I look at students as individuals.

WORKING WITH THE WHOLE GROUP

During a whole-group experience, everyone in the class receives explicit instruction and modeling at the same time, but because each child has different needs, the teacher asks different students to do different things based on ability.

Although whole-group instruction does work, this method of instruction should not be used for every interactive writing experience. Whole-group instruction is difficult for many teachers. I find that whenever a group's size increases, it becomes more difficult to monitor and engage all students in the experience, and fewer students are able to be involved in the writing process. Knowing your students is essential in order to get optimum benefits from the experience.

During a whole-group experience, I sit in a chair in front of my class, and the students sit near me on the carpet. To actively engage all students and provide added control, I distribute small, individual dry-erase/white boards or chalkboards; using individual writing materials allows students to be active participants even when it is not their turn to write on the group's paper. I find that a few students have trouble keeping up with the actual writing that is taking place, and working on individual dry-erase boards allows them to focus on a skill level that meets their own needs. Using this method also allows all students to practice different skills. For example, if students know only the beginning and ending sounds in a word, they are able to write them down on the dry-erase boards without fear of making a mistake or of being wrong. As students are able, they begin to practice hearing and writing what comes in the middle of a word.

Individual dry-erase boards are an easy way to give focused instruction in a specific area, such as letter formation, left- to-right progression, and beginning, middle, and end sounds, allowing me to monitor the students: I observe what the students are writing as they write along with the child working at the chart, and I can see who is having difficulties. The focus can be on specific words; I have students practice a specific word until they are able to write it smoothly and easily. While students are in a whole-group setting, the use of this added element may also lessen anxiety, while providing every student the opportunity to be successful.

Small dry-erase boards can be used differently in a whole-group setting depending on the students' needs. For example, when I want to focus on a specific skill or strategy that not all students do need, the focus group of students sits in the front. I give them each a different color marking pen, and they are the only ones allowed to verbally respond and participate in the actual writing of the text on the chart paper. (Using different color markers also allows me to easily monitor what each student contributes to a piece of writing.) The other students participate by working out words or sentences on their dry-erase boards. They show me their work by holding up their boards for me to read.

A Whole-Group Lesson. After I read many different versions of *The Three Little Pigs* to my students, we gathered together as a class on the carpet to reflect. In the stories I had read, the structure and the characters varied slightly, but the theme remained the same. As a whole class, we listed all the things that were the same in the versions. I find that creating lists as a whole-group experience is a wonderful source of ideas for future interactive writing lessons.

WORKING IN SMALL GROUPS

I often use interactive writing in a small-group setting. Small-group interactive writing provides an opportunity for more students to become actively engaged in the actual writing process. I have found that small groups are more focused, and I can tailor small-group experiences to meet the needs of the students in a particular group. When the group is small, students move faster because the lesson's focus is more directed.

Small groups also are easier to monitor than large groups. When I don't have to worry about engaging and providing means for a large group of students to participate actively, I am able to direct the lesson to my small group of students. This allows me to pull out students for specific teaching points. When scaffolding is done in this manner, children focus on the process, not the product.

Small groups are more mobile and need less space to work; they can easily work at a table or a small group of desks. They can also easily be incorporated into a class's guided reading or writer's workshop time.

Small groups have their drawbacks. For example, students may be grouped according to ability, which limits the writing they are able to do. Also, fewer ideas can be shared in small groups than in large groups.

Although small groups can be a wonderful avenue for explicit instruction, it does mean other children must also be provided with and engaged in other meaningful activities. To do this creates more work and preparation for me as the teacher.

A Small-Group Lesson. After discussing several versions of *The Three Little Pigs* and creating the lists to compare and contrast the stories in small groups, I presented a new version of the story. After giving a book talk and making predictions based on the students' prior knowledge of the characters and structure gleaned from the other versions of the story, I worked with small groups to write out a short paragraph that reflected the students' thoughts about the new version. Mai, excited and almost unable to contain himself, raises his hand just before he explodes, "I know, I know, I know, the first thing we need to write is the new story has three pigs, one wolf, and three houses." It is here that the negotiation begins. Working with the other students in the small group, we negotiate the text to be written. We work on fluency and phrasing together before actually writing. Small-group collaboration helps to create text that makes sense and is an important avenue that allows students to share ideas and strategies.

WORKING WITH PAIRS

Interactive writing can also be done in pairs. Pairs can consist of the teacher and a student or a weaker student working with a stronger classmate. Because students learn to write by writing, pairs should have different strengths or areas of need. Students work largely without teacher monitoring, so the writing may not always be done the way the teacher would like it; also, opportunities for generating and sharing ideas are more limited when only two students work together. Nevertheless, pairs are an excellent way to build self-esteem and a sense of cooperation, and they allow students to focus on individual needs. I often pair myself with a student; we negotiate the text together while sharing the pen. A pair of students who are creating a joint project can discuss effectively the language they will use in a piece of interactive writing.

A Paired Lesson. I also use *The Three Little Pigs* theme for paired writing activities. I work with a student to create a sentence about a book we have read. The student I've chosen to work with is Mary; she hears beginning and ending sounds, but has a difficult time hearing anything that comes in the middle of words, even though the other students in the class have already mastered this. By pulling Mary aside and working in a paired situation, I am able to work on this area in a safe, nonthreatening manner. Mary and I negotiate the sentence *The big bad wolf runs fast*. Mary hears some sounds, and we work together to write complete words for our sentence. Instead of *The bg bd wf rns ft*, we work until our completed sentence reads, *The big bad wolf runs fast*. Mary is successful.

I like paired writing experiences because I am able to address an individual student's area of need, while at the same time using the student's strengths to create a text that makes him or her feel successful.

CONCLUSION

Whole groups, small groups, or pairs of writers can accomplish tasks such as these:

- List making (grocery, things to do, names)
- Letter writing and cards to family and friends
- Notes and messages

- Sign making
- Invitations to parties
- Class rules
- Labels for the classroom
- Directions to make or do something
- Directions to get someplace
- Recording information
- Writing paragraphs
- Comparing and contrasting information
- Recording opinions
- Brainstorming solutions to problems
- Evaluating
- Gathering practical or factual information
- Making story maps, webs, Venn diagrams
- Retelling a story
- Speech bubbles

When I use interactive writing as a tool for learning, each experience must be carefully planned to ensure success. It is essential to look at the group setting, size, and composition. Figure 3 summarizes interactive writing group considerations.

Interactive writing provides an authentic means for literacy instruction. I have found that by carefully grouping those students requiring additional instruction, they are better able to receive appropriate and ample support in order to be successful.

GROUP SIZE	BENEFITS	DIFFICULTIES

Whole Group	Provides opportunities for:
	- Planning and
	  constructing text
	- Demonstrating concepts and
	  skills to all students
	- Whole-class exposure to
	  words and concepts
	- Students share information
		Students may be overlooked.
		
		Students may find it easier to get lost in the group.
		
		The ability to control and monitor all students in the group decreases.
		
		Fewer students are involved in the actual writing process.
		
		More supplies are needed.

Small Group	Provides opportunities for:
	- Planning and
	  constructing text
	- Demonstrating concepts/
	  skills as needed to focus
	  groups of students
	- More students to become
	  involved in the writing process
	  limiting the writing.
	- Connecting writing directly to
	  students' interests
	
	Easier to pinpoint student's area(s) of need.
	
	Controling and monitoring students are not as difficult as in a large-group setting.
	
	Fewer materials and less space are needed.
		Not as many ideas are shared as with the whole group.
		
		There may not be as much verbalization.
		
		Students may be grouped according to ability,

Pairs	Provides oppurtunities for: - Planning and constructing text - Building self-esteem - Working with peers - One-on-one experiences - Focus on individual needs	Ideas and sharing are limited. Writing may not be done the way the teacher would like it to be done.

FIGURE 3 Interactive writing group considerations.

BUILDING ON EVERY CHILD'S FAVORITE WORD

Carolyn Stewart

Teaching letter identification and sound recognition can be very frustrating. This is especially true when working with children who have limited background knowledge and children who are English language learners (ELLs). Traditional strategies often fail to actively engage these children. I have tried many new strategies hoping to discover a method that would really benefit my struggling learners. You can imagine my delight when I recognized two resources that had been in my classroom just waiting to be discovered: children's favorite word (in other words, their name), and interactive writing. Combining these two resources creates a powerful learning strategy not only for my struggling learners but for all learners.

I reflected on my observations of children and their names. The first word that many children learn to read and write is their name. I considered what happens when I call a child by the wrong name: Most are very displeased and correct my error immediately! Their strong identity to their name creates a powerful, natural, and highly motivating learning tool. I knew that integrating the children's names with interactive writing would only increase the power of the shared pen.

In this chapter, I share two interactive writing activities that I use. Both activities are centered on the child's name. They are designed to actively engage all children in meaningful learning experiences. I use the first activity, creating a class chart, as a whole-group activity. The second activity, creating a class-made book, is a one-to-one activity in which I work with one student at a time to write a sentence for the book. Included in this chapter are some warm-up activities that I have adapted from Patricia Cunningham (2002), which I use to prepare the children for interactive writing.

I introduce these name activities in the first quarter of the school year to help the children get acquainted with one another. I use them as one of the children's first one-to-one interactive writing experiences. Because their name is the subject of the sentence, they are excited about writing and are less intimidated by the writing process. For a classroom of 20 children, it takes about a month for everyone to have a turn. I have found it time well spent.

WARM-UP ACTIVITIES

Before I engage the children in interactive writing, I use several warm-up activities that prepare the children for writing.

M	a	r	i	a							
C	h	r	i	s	t	o	p	h	e	r	
P	a	n	h	i	a						
K	a	t	i	e							
T	i	m	m	y							
G	a	o									
A	l	e	j	a	n	d	r	o			
J	u	n	i	o	r						
P	a	b	l	o							
S	h	a	y	l	e	n	e				
T	h	y									
D	e	v	o	n	t	e					
J	a	n	e	t							

FIGURE 4 Class name graph.

Focus Name. I use one child's name as the focus for the day's learning activities. I often use the name of the helper for the day as the focus name. I begin this whole-group activity by writing the focus name on two sentence strips; I leave one name strip intact and cut the other between the letters to form letter cards. The children show me where to make the cuts. I put the name strip in the pocket chart and mix the letter cards. Then the children take turns "spelling" the name by matching the letter cards with the name strip in the pocket chart. I point out that this name is a word and that it can be this word only if the letters are in the correct order.

While the name is still in the pocket chart, I begin a discussion of the concepts I want to emphasize. Some possibilities include: discussing the first letter; noting the letter name, letter sound, and that it is a capital letter; discovering other names that begin with the same letter and letter sound; counting the letters in the name; and checking for identical letters. After we complete this discussion, the intact name strip is added to the classroom word wall.

Class Graph. I list the child's name on a class graph made from graph paper with 1-inch squares, as shown in Figure 4. I have the children help me "spell" the name as I write each letter in a square going across the graph paper. Each focus name, in turn, is added to the graph. As I add the focus name, I lead the children to make observations about the names listed, reinforcing the previous discussion. Questions may include: How many letters in the name? Which names begin with the same letter? If some begin with the same letter, how can we tell the names apart? Who has the longest/shortest name?

INTERACTIVE WRITING ACTIVITIES

I am now ready to guide the children to the two interactive writing activities. I begin the first activity by modeling good writing and then leading the children into the interactive writing process.

Creating a Personal Chart. The class creates a personal chart for a child. This child sits in the teacher's chair and is interviewed by the class. Initially, I model appropriate questioning techniques, but soon the children take over the interviewing process. Some questions the children might ask are: Do you have any pets? What is your favorite movie? What game do you like to play? What is your favorite food? As the child responds to the classmates' questions, I record the answers on the chart.

After I have written the responses to four or five questions, I give the children a chance to share the pen. I ask the children to tell a kind sentence about the child we interviewed. Examples might be: Maria is a good friend. Maria is a hard worker. Maria is kind. The class chooses a sentence to write together. I help the children determine the number of words to be written by holding up a finger for each word spoken. Beginning with the first word, I make a line for each letter in the word. For *Maria*, I make five short lines like this: _ _ _ _ _. I then invite Maria to write her name on the lines. After I write the lines for the next word, we orally stretch the word, saying it very slowly, listening for the individual phonemes. I select a volunteer to write the word with a colored pen. I support the child's writing by stretching the word again or writing unknown letters with the black pen. We read what has been written, and then we continue the process until the sentence is completed. I always have 1-inch correction tape available during interactive writing. The child places a piece over an incorrect letter and writes on top of the tape. I call it "magic tape" because it makes mistakes disappear.

I now use the completed chart for further teaching points, or we can revisit it at a later time. It is an excellent tool for teaching concepts about print. I ask the children to use their hands to frame a letter or a word to check their understanding of *letter* and *word*. I invite the children to frame the space between words to demonstrate the concept of *word*. I have the children point to the period, question mark, or exclamation mark to teach punctuation. We reread the chart together to demonstrate top-to-bottom progression, left-to-right progression, and return sweep. I also use the chart as an opportunity to introduce high-frequency words that are evident in the chart text.

Class-Made Book. The final activity is to create a class-made book based on the personal chart for the child to take home. During free flow center time, I invite one child at a time to come sit with me to use interactive writing to complete a sentence for a page in the book. Depending on the child's ability level, I have him or her write a whole sentence or complete a cloze. I invite children who need less support to tell me a sentence about the child. We then begin writing the sentence using the same interactive writing process described for the whole-group activity. Figure 5 is an example of a child-made sentence.

For children needing more support, I offer a cloze to help them write their sentence. We reread the chart and select a sentence or an idea that the child can use in completing the cloze. An example of a cloze I might use is _____ likes to _____. The completed cloze might read: <u>Maria</u> likes to <u>eat pizza</u>. Another cloze I might use is _____ favorite _____ is _____. The completed cloze might read: <u>Maria's</u> favorite <u>color</u> is <u>blue</u>. Figure 6 is an example of a child's completed cloze. I have found that using a cloze to complete the sentence provides the necessary support for ELL students. Because we reread the chart together, it is not necessary for ELL children to generate a complete sentence on their own. The chart provides the sentence or idea that ELL children can use in completing the cloze.

FIGURE 5 Child-made sentence for the class-made book.

FIGURE 6 Child's completed cloze sentence.

After the children complete their sentence, they go to a nearby table to draw a picture to match their sentence. I can usually have 8 to 10 children complete a page during center time. I bind the completed pages together and read the book to the whole class. I then send the book home with the child.

CONCLUSION

Combining the use of children's names and interactive writing is an exciting learning tool in my classroom. Every child, regardless of ability level or language experience, is successful in these activities. The children exhibit a high level of enthusiasm for the activities and demonstrate a keen sense of ownership for the finished product. The finished product is useful in teaching concepts about print and letter and sound recognition in a real-world context. Best of all, I enjoy using children's names as a natural introduction to one-to-one interactive writing. The children's first experience with interactive writing is so positive that they are eager to continue writing both with me and independently. My hope is that you will use some or all of these activities to begin building on every child's favorite word.

REFERENCE

Cunningham, P. M. (2002). *Phonics they use: Words for reading and writing* (3rd ed.). New York: HarperCollins.

Environmental Print: Building a Bridge to Literacy

*Diane Leonard and
Stephanie Collom*

Children begin recognizing familiar signs and symbols at an early age, long before they can read print. Fast-food logos and traffic signs are often among the first connections to literacy that young children make. They are the first understanding children develop that abstract symbols convey meaning.

One of the best ways that teachers can support emergent readers and writers is by saturating their classrooms with environmental print; everything from cereal box labels to soda cans can become sources of authentic text working as conduits to literacy. Early readers and writers can also access meaning through other types of environmental print, such as student and class projects.

According to Irene Fountas and Gay Su Pinnell (1996, p. 43), "A classroom organized for literacy learning invites children to use print in purposeful ways; wherever possible, written language—materials for reading and writing—are incorporated naturally and authentically . . . the setting is safe and supportive and enables all learners to develop confidence, take risks, learn to work independently, and develop social skills." Incorporating interactive writing with environmental print supports this kind of literacy environment. Interactive writing provides students with the chance to apply their knowledge of sound/symbol relationships at their own developmental levels. By participating in interactive writing opportunities, students begin to learn the power of the pen; they share the role of scribe in writing experiences over which they gain complete ownership.

Completed interactive writing projects can be added to the print displayed around the classroom; students build literacy skills by revisiting these finished pieces during literacy centers or further learning activities. Literacy centers are meaningful and functional genuine language activities in which students are encouraged to "listen, talk, read, write, view, or create visual representations" (Tompkins, 2002, p. 42).

There are several types of interactive writing projects that lend themselves to becoming part of a classroom's environmental print, including making words, writing narratives, and writing expository texts.

MAKING WORDS

Activities involving the making of words are most appropriate for emergent readers and writers. Attention is paid to combining letters and sounds to create individual words for various purposes. "Children's understanding of the concept of a 'word' is an important part of becoming literate" (Tompkins, 2002, p. 144). Children's own names are a good way to start because these words are very meaningful to children. They are excited about learning how to write the word that represents them. Turn to "Building on Every Child's Favorite Word" on p. 14 to read about interactive writing and using children's names.

Word Banks. Writing student names interactively on cards is an effective first word bank experience for beginning readers and writers. The name card can then be matched with student photos as a purposeful reading activity. Children enjoy matching names with their classmates' pictures. When the cards are placed together in a pocket chart as a literacy center, the matching activity becomes a meaningful one with which students can interact without teacher intervention. Other word banks can be written interactively as well. Some suggestions include: sight words, vocabulary, thematic, and monthly word banks.

Key Words. Key words are personalized, high-interest words that students identify based on their interests; they serve as personalized dictionaries because students create their own lists of words. Key words can be written interactively one-on-one with students and attached to book rings for them to use during independent or group writing activities. Key word rings may also serve as a source of meaningful reading material for students.

Labeling. Labels facilitate understanding of concepts and artifacts and can be especially important for students learning to speak English. When students help to write the labels for articles in the classroom, they attach more ownership to learning the names for items in class.

Labels can include student names and the names of classroom objects. When added to calendars, labels help students note important dates such as birthdays, holidays, and special events. Labels can also be attached to learning charts and artwork. They are particularly useful in the area of science; labels can highlight anatomical features of organisms displayed on life science charts, as seen in Figure 7.

Classroom learning charts and displays of realia for concepts such as the solar system, the water cycle, and volcanism become more valuable when students have

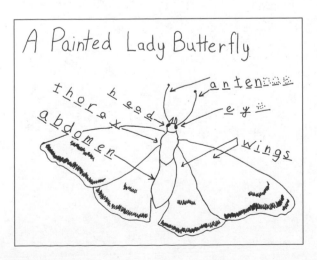

FIGURE 7 Labels on a life science chart.

helped create the labels and the explanatory text attached to them. Students tend to learn key vocabulary words or terminology more readily when they are involved in the label-writing process. They also return to the completed displays of interactively written texts as they read or write in the room during literacy center time.

Interactively written labels are also helpful when attached to artwork. Features of the work may be better revealed by providing labels and/or accompanying explanatory text. Students viewing the piece can read labels containing information such as the artist's name, subject, medium, and technique, which facilitate understanding and appreciation of the completed artwork.

Lists. Making lists is another authentic reason for students to participate in interactive writing. For example, shopping lists can be generated in preparation for a cooking experience in class. Writing the shopping list together with the teacher allows children a window into the teacher's thoughts concerning the cooking lesson.

Lists are a good way for students to organize information and can be used for many purposes during instruction. One way of utilizing list making is during thematic instruction. For example, during a thematic science unit about trees, kindergarten children can help to write a list of products that come from trees, as shown in Figure 8. The types of lists generated in a classroom are limited only by the teacher's and the students' imaginations.

To Do lists allow children to see how grown-ups organize their time. They are a good model of priority setting for students. To Do lists may be preparation lists showing what a teacher needs to accomplish in preparation for a learning activity or a special school event. Older students can be taught to make To Do lists for themselves to organize their day or week at school.

Supply lists can be written as well; these lists can appear at work stations around the classroom. Students can refer to them to make sure they have the materials needed for successful completion of the activity at the station. Lists enable students to take

FIGURE 8 List of products that come from trees.

over more responsibility for keeping learning supplies neat and orderly. Placing a supply list near the storage area for P.E. and playground equipment helps students keep better track of the equipment. Students enjoy the feeling of responsibility that working with supply lists engenders, and teachers enjoy being able to transfer the attention they would normally have to give to inventorying supplies in other directions.

A list of attributes can be written interactively. Descriptive words naming the attributes of animate or inanimate objects helps children see them in more detail and understand them more fully. Attribute lists are good vehicles for expanding vocabulary. For example, the sentence frame "A pig is _____" helps students create a list of words that describe a pig.

Students can also list the attributes of characters from stories they have read. During a thematic fairy tale unit, students may learn that certain attributes relate to certain character types: Villains are usually ugly and evil, and they persecute the heroes, who are usually attractive and noble, and who overcome obstacles to achieve their rewards. Listing character attributes, as shown in Figure 9, allows students, especially English language learners, to better understand literary characters and expand their descriptions of them. Students learn that characters are more complex than simply good or bad.

WRITING NARRATIVES

By listing attributes of characters during interactive writing activities, students develop a better sense of how characters function in stories. They are able to make more informed predictions about the characters they encounter while reading stories.

Graphic Organizers. Graphic organizers are a wonderful way of organizing information. When they are used in conjunction with interactive writing during language

FIGURE 9 List of character attributes.

arts, math, and science activities, students are more likely to understand and remember the information they contain. They are also more likely to revisit the completed graphic organizers for different purposes during literacy center time. Graphic organizers come in all kinds of shapes and sizes; some of the most versatile and frequently used are Venn diagrams, graphs, concept clusters or webs, KWL charts, story maps, sequence flow charts, character analysis charts, and cyclical charts.

Venn diagrams function well in any activity where attention is to be paid to the similarities and differences between two individuals or groups. One highly effective use of Venn diagrams is in noting similarities and differences between stories or characters. Two stories our students enjoy comparing are *Patrick's Dinosaurs*, by Carol Carrick (1983), and *The Trek*, by Ann Jonas (1985).

The two stories are alike in many ways. Both stories involve two characters imagining different animals as they take a walk; but there are some major differences that students enjoy noting as well. Our students are usually very eager to spend a considerable amount of time analyzing story contents for inclusion on the diagram.

Different versions of a folktale such as *The Three Little Pigs* and a newer version of the story such as the *Three Little Wolves and the Big Bad Pig* (Trivizas, 1993) can be compared very effectively using Venn diagrams. When comparing different versions of a story, students begin to see a writing formula at work. Once they learn the formula used to write the original story and subsequent versions by other authors, they welcome the opportunity to create classroom story versions of their own.

Literacy Centers. Literacy centers are meaningful, functional, and genuine language activities that provide students the opportunity to practice and interact with language through reading, writing, listening, speaking, viewing, and visual representation experiences (Tompkins, 2002). Interactive writing has a valuable role in classroom literacy centers. All literacy center activities should be introduced and practiced with the whole class before being placed in literacy centers for independent practice.

Language activities such as word building, poetry, onsets and rimes, and interactive charts can be included in literacy centers. Interactive charts are poetry, song, or cloze sentence charts on which key phrases or words can be attached with velcro dots. The velcroed text pieces can be removed and interchanged with other pieces, as shown in Figure 10. At the listening center, teachers can provide copies of student or class-authored stories or texts that have been created using interactive writing in large-group, small-group, or individual settings. The completed text may be recorded by teachers or other students and then be placed together with the written work at the listening center where it can be enjoyed by all.

Projects that have been written interactively, such as laminated big books, class-authored books, and murals and charts, can be placed in the writing center as a source of ideas for independent writing projects. Children may use water-based markers to circle consonant blends, divide compound words, break longer words into decodable "chunks," and identify small words contained in larger words. They can document their work on small chalkboards or dry-erase boards, in writing center journals, or on special note pads of paper. When their work is completed, they simply erase using a wet sponge or remove their journals or papers, and the center is ready for the next set of students.

Interactively written stories may be displayed as wall stories or story quilts before they are bound and placed at the classroom's big book center. Class innovations of children's literature, described in "Setting Sail on a Sea of Words: A Passage Into Story Innovations" on p. 45, make meaningful additions to the center; students enjoy reading them independently or with classmates. Students also enjoy taking the written big books to other classrooms and administrative offices to read and share them with the school community at large. Interactively written daily news journals can be revisited during literacy center time; students

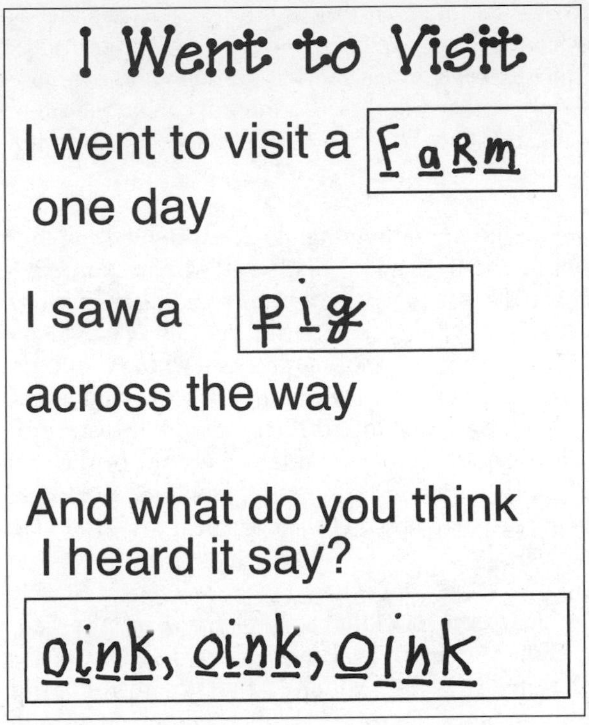

I Went to Visit

I went to visit a [FaRm] one day

I saw a [pig]

across the way

And what do you think I heard it say?

[oink, oink, oink]

FIGURE 10 Interactive chart with removable text.

can reread and add to previous journal entries. They may elect to copy the text and take it home to share with their families.

EXPOSITORY ENVIRONMENTAL PRINT

Interactive writing can have an important role in expository writing in the classroom. Students can conduct research and the text can be written interactively and displayed in the room with accompanying illustrations. Many materials that are usually teacher made or purchased can be written interactively with the students and displayed in the classroom for student use.

Alphabet Lines. At the beginning of the school year, teachers can have young children help write the classroom alphabet line instead of displaying a commercially produced alphabet line purchased from a teacher supply store. Students take turns interactively writing the capital and lowercase letters for inclusion on the classroom alphabet line. Writing the letters, drawing corresponding illustrations, and then placing them correctly on the classroom alphabet line help kindergartners and first graders understand where the letters appear in the alphabet. Teachers are also able to observe students as they form the letters. Meaningful handwriting lessons can become natural outgrowths from the context of the larger alphabet line writing lessons. It makes for a meaningful and purposeful introduction or review of letters and sounds.

Students remember and can identify letters and sounds because they assume responsibility for writing the letters and drawing the corresponding pictures that appear on the alphabet strip. Students learn in a more natural setting that there is a correct way letters are formed.

While observing students writing letters, teachers are able to make on-the-spot assessments of fine motor skill development. Interactive writing is a good instrument for teachers to use to evaluate handwriting ability. As teachers focus on the letters a child is writing , they can see whether the child can form the letters correctly. Letter reversals and incorrect use of capitals can also be seen and evaluated. Students making the same types of mistakes in letter formation can subsequently be pulled aside for minilessons based on handwriting needs assessed during the interactive writing process.

Field Trips. Field trips are a good source of meaningful expository writing in the classroom. Photographs taken during the trip can be displayed with accompanying interactively written labels. They can also be placed in a book retelling the field trip experience in which the text is written interactively. Field trip retelling can also be done on charts. The teacher and students can work together as a whole group or in small-group settings to retell the events of the trip sequentially. When this activity is done in small groups, the class can be broken into three groups, with each group taking one section of the field trip sequence. Each student member of the small groups can choose a "signature color"; by having each student select a color with which to write and sign their names, the teacher can tell at a glance what the young authors are able to do for themselves.

Recipes. Recipes used during classroom cooking activities are another good vehicle for interactive writing, as shown in Figure 11. Helping to write a recipe gives students practice in giving directions. It is also valuable practice in following a sequence or series of steps. If the finished recipe is duplicated and sent home,

FIGURE 11 Recipe written interactively.

students make the real-life connection between their recipe steps and application outside of the school learning environment.

Artwork. When artwork is completed in the style or manner of a famous master artist, students can help research the artist and write his or her biography interactively. Learning and writing about the artist help students gain a deeper understanding and appreciation of the artist's life and work. Directions telling how the student artwork was created can be posted next to the finished student pieces for viewers of the completed work to read. Students learn that communicating the how-to steps enables other people to repeat them in a similar project.

Other Projects. Classroom projects involving the construction of habitats or other living environments such as a pond provide students authentic reasons to label and write about the project interactively. They can describe the creative process used during construction of the project or tell about the creatures living in the habitat. Teachers may have students include information found during research activities.

Retellings of other classroom learning experiences such as visits by guest speakers and presenters from the surrounding community can be described meaningfully using interactive writing. They can then be displayed on the classroom walls to be read later by students. Retellings provide good opportunities to practice describing sequence and content.

Every interactive writing experience provides wonderful opportunities to incorporate skill instruction within the context of an authentic writing activity. Possible prompts for teachers to use during meaningful interactive writing lessons that target specific skill instruction are given in Figure 12.

FIGURE 12 Prompts for use with interactive writing.

- How many words do you hear?
- Stretch the word. What sound do you hear at the beginning (next, end)?
- Why do we need a space?
- Should we use a capital or lowercase letter? Why?
- Reread with me from the beginning. What comes next?
- What do we need at the end?
- Let's count and point to the words.
- Can someone come and show me a . . . letter, word (any word), space, capital letter, a particular letter, sight word, etc.
- Come up and show me (or underline, draw a box around, highlight, etc.) a word that starts with . . . (letter).
- Show me a word that ends with . . . (letter).
- Show me a word that begins (or ends) like . . . (say a word).
- Show me a word that rhymes with . . . .
- Find the word that has the same vowel sound as . . . .
- Find the word that has the . . . sound.
- Frame a word where the "r" changes the vowel sound.
- Find the word that has an ending that changes the word to mean more than one.
- Show me a compound word. Circle the two words.
- Find the word . . . . Circle the root word.
- Find the word that means . . . . What other word could we have used?
- Show me the word . . . . Let's clap the syllables.
- Find a word that has . . . syllables.
- Show me a describing (action, naming) word.
- What pronoun could we use in place of "John"?

CONCLUSION

"In reading, children move from recognizing environmental print in the world around them to reading decontextualized words in books. . . . Researchers have found that young emergent readers depend on context to read familiar words and memorized texts. . . . Slowly, children develop relationships linking form and meaning as they learn concepts about written language and gain more experience reading and writing" (Tompkins, 2002, pp. 144–145). Interactive writing helps young children make the transition from squiggle and picture writing to more conventional forms of writing. It functions as a scaffold supporting the writing abilities of older students. When interactive writing is incorporated into the environmental print in a classroom, it becomes a tremendously powerful bridge to literacy.

REFERENCES

Carrick, C. (1983). *Patrick's dinosaurs*. New York: Houghton Mifflin.

Fountas, I. C., & Pinnell, G. S. (1996). *Guided reading*. Portsmouth, NH: Heinemann.

Jonas, A. (1985). *The trek*. New York: Macmillan.

Tompkins, G. (2002). *Language arts: Content and teaching strategies* (5th ed.). Upper Saddle River, NJ: Merrill/Prentice Hall.

Trivizas, E. (1993). *The three little wolves and the big bad pig*. New York: Macmillan.

WONDER WALLS: CREATING RESEARCH MURALS WITH YOUNG CHILDREN

Diane Leonard

Interactive writing has developed a very high profile in my classroom over the last couple of years. It has proven to be one of the most versatile and effective tools in my teaching tool kit. I began by simply incorporating interactive writing into my class's Daily News journal at the end of the day. As I became more comfortable with the mechanics of the interactive writing process, I began to see how it could be implemented effectively in various ways throughout other content areas. Slowly but surely, I began to weave interactive writing opportunities throughout the school day.

I'd begun to incorporate interactive writing in the area of science. My first-grade students and I started by using interactive writing while developing word banks, labels, and learning charts for whichever science unit we were working on. As the year progressed, I saw how interactive writing could also be utilized during the creation of research murals.

Research murals are wall murals containing nonfiction text and illustrations generated by students. The information displayed on the murals is derived from hands-on science explorations and observations and information gleaned from print media related to a thematic unit. Completed murals can be hung around the classroom, where students can read and share the informational text they have helped to research and write.

The research murals my students made were culminating activities related to extended thematic learning experiences in the areas of earth and life science. Students who were involved in making the murals understood clearly that their interactively written mural panels exhibited writing used for authentic communication purposes. The murals documented the understanding of concepts learned while students were engaged in meaningful scientific exploration and discovery.

OUR INTERACTIVE WRITING PROCESS

My students and I used the same interactive writing procedure in completing the text for our murals as for writing our classroom's daily news. Because the technique is the same for both projects, a description of the procedure may be helpful in understanding how we completed the text for our murals.

Each afternoon, before they are dismissed for the day, my students and I reflect on the day's activities and learning experiences. After some discussion, the class helper of the day dictates the news for the day that will be recorded in our Daily News Journal. Because most of my students are learning English as a second language, a bit of fine-tuning, offered either by more English-proficient students or by me, is often needed to make our entry grammatically correct. The students and I then recite the agreed-upon sentence together, using our fingers to count the number of words we will need to keep track of during the interactive writing process. We also review conventions of print as needed.

Students take turns writing the words of the sentence, one word per child. As the sentence is assembled, the class returns to the beginning of the sentence and practices reading the text up to the most recent word addition. We always verify that we have the correct number of words before we add the punctuation at the end. Then we read the completed sentence a final time.

If children are able to spell a word independently, I encourage them to do so. If a child is unsure, I draw small letter lines, one for each letter of the word the child is attempting to spell. For example, if, the student is unsure of the spelling of "friend", I use my black "teacher marker" to draw __ __ __ __ __ __. Everyone says the word aloud while using their hands to stretch the word. The idea behind stretching the word orally is to help students listen for letter sounds they may need as they attempt to spell the word. The word is usually written in sequence from left to right. I supply the letters the student scribe doesn't know. When the word is completed, we circle any consonant blend that is at the beginning of the word; in *friend*, we circle the *fr*. When this is done consistently over a long period of time, young readers and writers begin to develop the understanding that some phonemes, or sounds, are represented by two or more letters. The letter lines help underscore the point.

Students begin to notice other spelling conventions as well. If every letter sound is accounted for in the word but one letter line is left blank at the end of the word, students quickly catch on that it must be for silent *e*.

Letter lines also reinforce directionality as well as allow the child to see the length of the word. Beginning writers often need such reinforcement. Letter lines are a concrete reminder that words are written from left to right. Children learn to use the letter lines as anchor points that help them focus on how long the word being written is going to be. In counting the number of letter lines I write for them, students can begin to zero in on the letters and sounds they need to think about and listen for as they write their words.

Although most students generally write their words from left to right, some students prefer to place the initial and final letters on the appropriate letter lines before attempting to fill in the remaining letters in the middle of the word. As they become more comfortable with their writing successes, these students generally make a natural shift over to the more conventional left-to-right sequential spelling used by their peers. The initial/final-letter-first approach is a temporary stage for some students, helping them to see a word's finiteness in a more concrete way.

RESEARCH MURALS

This basic procedure became so successful with my students that I began to use it in every curricular area. The idea of using the procedure for murals grew out of a workshop I attended in January of 1998 that was presented by San Joaquin Valley Writing Project Teacher Consultant Terry Kasner. I was amazed to see the research she had been able to do with her kindergartners. She demonstrated how her students could group life science pictures using sorting mats labeled with particular topic headings to facilitate discussion and the research process. She showed how to help students organize picture data based on their observations of the pictures. She also included information about helping older students with research projects. She dealt with the specter of plagiarism by teaching students in first grade and beyond to copy no more than three key words at a time of text found in books. Students were then taught how to restate those key words in their own words.

I left the workshop excited about the idea of trying research with my own first graders. I began to think of ways to include interactive writing in the process.

I decided that I would combine Terry's data gathering and sorting activities with the wall stories I was already creating with my students. My students had a great deal of practice with making innovations of favorite trade books in long, paneled strips known as wall stories. They enjoyed reading the walls around the room. I decided to use informational text the students researched in the same wall story format, and research murals were born.

Earth Science Mural. Our first mural was titled "Pebbles, Sand, and Silt." The title was the same as that of the first-grade earth science unit I was teaching at the time. The mural was divided into three panels, one for pebbles, one for sand, and one for silt. Information the students gathered and discovered during the course of the unit was written on the panels using interactive writing.

Students had access to rock and mineral picture books and real earth materials during the unit. Unit activities included observing and describing three types of rock under wet and dry conditions. Students brainstormed descriptive words as a whole group, and we wrote them interactively on a word bank chart. They also observed and described the particles of stone that could be rubbed from the three rock types, noting which types were the easiest and hardest to obtain particle samples from. We wrote their findings interactively on a separate Discovery chart used for documenting the discoveries they made while participating in unit activities.

Further activities included sifting pebbles through several sizes of mesh screen to separate pebbles into five size categories—large, medium, and small pebbles, gravel, and sand. Once sand was separated from the mix, students placed sand samples into vials and added water. The vials were shaken, and students discovered a layer of silt on top of the sand once all the particles sifted to the bottom of the vials. Students learned that clay used in making many different types of products comes from silt. The unit concluded with investigating the ways people use the earth materials studied in the unit. Each activity added new findings to our word bank and Discovery chart.

I asked students to generate sentences for the culminating research mural project based on their observations, their experiences, information on the Discovery chart, and ideas found in books related to the theme. We worked for several days as a whole group using interactive writing to produce the text for each of the three mural panels. One of the panels is shown in Figure 13.

Students volunteered ideas and sentences for the mural. For this first mural, the teacher made especially sure that students drew pictures of things mentioned in the text.

The students were very proud of their newly acquired knowledge and enjoyed sharing the mural with their parents during Open House. Parents were surprised at the depth of learning students demonstrated through their writing.

FIGURE 13 Completed panel from science mural.

Life Science. Recently, my class learned about frogs and toads during a unit for life science. The topic lent itself very well to making a research mural. The development of the mural was more complex than the process used earlier in the year during construction of the Pebbles, Sand, and Silt mural.

The mural was again to be a culminating activity for the thematic unit. During the unit, students had ample opportunities to read and listen to froggy stories through books and audiotapes. There was plenty of information for them to learn from nonfiction books, videos, and a live tadpole habitat.

The tadpole habitat was set up in the classroom science learning center. Consisting of a fish tank filled with pond water, freshwater snails, tadpoles, and live plants, the tadpole habitat soon became the most popular area in the classroom. Magnifying lenses, observation journals, frog metamorphosis pictures, frog books, and writing supplies were also present at the center to assist young scientists in collecting data about frogs. Students also participated in many learning activities integrated throughout the curriculum content areas that broadened the background knowledge they needed to complete the mural. It was important to provide my English language learners with a great deal of linguistic support through my bilingual instructional assistant as well.

For this research mural project, I decided to concentrate on the topic areas of frog habitat, diet, reproduction, and interesting facts. Students were asked to choose which topic area they wanted to work on. They had helped create a similar mural earlier in the year during a study of the life cycle of a butterfly, but this mural would be the first time they worked in small groups based on their topic area of interest.

When I was certain that students had developed enough background knowledge for them to be successful with the project, we began. First, the students gathered in a large circle on the carpet. I explained that they were going to be making a new mural about frogs, but that because they were now mural "experts," they would be making more of the decisions about how to construct the mural than in previous projects.

I began a discussion about where students could find useful information. Using shared writing, with me acting as the scribe, the students helped brainstorm a list of good sources. Ideas included "in our heads," "in books," "the tadpole habitat," and "on bulletin boards." I praised their responses and suggested that we concentrate on books as information sources first.

The students helped collect all the frog books from around the classroom. We stacked them in a big pile in the center of our discussion circle. Students were able to tell me that not every book would be good candidates for research. They thought that the best places to find real information about frogs would be in the "true" books. That idea led to a minilesson on the difference between fact and fiction. Students then helped sort the stack of books into a pile of fiction and a pile of nonfiction books. Students had very strong feelings about why a book fit in one of the two piles. It was very interesting listening to them talk to each other as they defended their reasoning. The hot topic under debate was that some of the fictional books had factual information. The students came to a quick agreement that they needed a third pile for these crossover books. By the time the discussion was finished, students were so entrenched in their sorting decisions that they requested that each group of books be displayed in a different location around the classroom.

We also conducted the next few mural production meetings as a whole group. The focus of the activities was to have students spend time researching by looking through informational texts for important pictures and ideas about what frogs eat, frog family life, interesting facts, and frog habitat. I encouraged students to share information with the class either by talking about the pictures or by reading parts of the text; this allowed students to participate at their own reading levels.

At the conclusion of the 2-day research sessions, the students used ideas and pictures from the books to generate sentences that were written interactively on a chart, as shown in Figure 14. The purpose of this activity was to have students

FIGURE 14 Frog facts written interactively on a chart.

practice writing ideas they found in the books in their own words. The finished chart was later displayed on the classroom wall for students to read as they read the room during literacy center time. It also appeared during guided reading time as a source for reading skill minilessons.

The next step in the research process was for students to choose which topic area they wanted to work on. The four topics that appeared at the tops of four large paper panels were: Habitat (part a in Figure 15), Food (part b in Figure 15), Family Life (part c in Figure 15), and Interesting Facts (part d in Figure 15). Once the students selected a topic they were interested in researching, the mural production process switched to small-group work to create each panel for the frog mural.

Over the course of several days, topic groups met with me one at a time to find information in books that was relevant to their topic. Each student then inter-actively wrote a sentence with me on a sentence strip in his or her own words that would be placed on the appropriate mural panel. Each student in the groups chose a different color of marker for his or her sentence. They signed their names with the same colors so that I could tell at a glance who had written which sentence. I could easily see what each child had been able to do independently. The marker colors were helpful to me as I assessed students' writing abilities.

Once the sentence strips were attached to the mural panels, it was time to begin the illustrations. On previous murals, students worked together to make illustrations. This time, they were insistent that each child would make his or her own for the frog mural. I believe they felt so much ownership of the decision making and content of the mural that it was important to them to make their own illustrations that, in their minds at least, matched their sentences.

After all the student artists were satisfied that their illustrations were complete, the four panels were taped together with clear book tape. The finished mural was displayed on the wall for all to read and admire. The students and I celebrated each child's achievement.

Although the completed mural wouldn't win any prizes for beauty, my students were very excited about "their" frog mural. It quickly became the favorite reading source in the classroom. They had a more powerful feeling of ownership for this mural than for any other. Every student could read his or her own work and explain the pictures. Some students could read part or all of the mural. Each student was able to enjoy the completed mural at his or her own level. That reason alone made the mural a truly beautiful creation.

When interest waned, I separated the panels and had them laminated. I used the panels as authentic sources for minilessons on the reading strategies word chunking and finding little words inside larger words. Students used overhead projector markers to separate word chunks or circle the little words. I scanned the student-authored text for every teachable point I could find. By the time we finished the mini-lessons, every child could read the entire mural. I placed the laminated panels back on the wall. The mural became a popular literacy center where student "teachers" could use markers and pens to teach their own minilessons to one another. They really enjoyed hunting for consonant blends and little words inside words.

Frogs <u>live</u> in the <u>water</u>.

Red-Eyed Tree Frogs <u>live</u> in trees.
<u>Some</u> <u>frogs</u> are <u>red</u>. <u>They</u> <u>live</u> in <u>rain forests</u>.

a

Frogs <u>eat</u> butterflies.
A <u>frog</u> <u>might</u> <u>eat</u> an <u>earthworm</u>.
<u>Some</u> <u>frogs</u> can <u>eat</u> <u>mice</u>.
A <u>frog</u> can <u>eat</u> <u>flies</u>.

b

<u>Mother</u> <u>frogs</u> <u>lay</u> <u>eggs in the water</u>.
<u>Tadpoles</u> <u>can</u> <u>swim</u>.
<u>Tadpoles</u> <u>hatch</u> <u>from</u> <u>frog eggs</u>.
<u>Tadpoles</u> <u>can</u> <u>change</u> <u>to</u> <u>be</u> <u>frogs</u>.

c

Frogs <u>lay</u> <u>eggs</u> in the <u>water</u>
Frogs can <u>jump far</u>.
A <u>male frog</u> has a vocal bag to call his female
I learned that when frogs lay
          eggs, they put jelly on them.

d

FIGURE 15 Four mural panel topics.

CONCLUSION

I am fortunate to have graduated along with my students to second grade for the following school year. We will continue to create more research murals in the future. I will act more in the role of facilitator, while students take on even more of the responsibilities for production. They will participate in more complex research activities and skills along the way.

The skills they acquire during the production of research murals will serve them well as they move on to higher grade levels. From making research murals, students have the background they will need to successfully write individual reports and papers once they journey beyond the walls of my classroom.

Weekly News: Beyond Show and Tell

Cynthia Schaefer

I began using interactive writing in conjunction with a "daily news" activity in my kindergarten classroom about 9 years ago. I began with the traditional concept of "show and tell" or "sharing" where students took turns standing in front of the class holding some object they had chosen to bring to school to "show" the rest of the class. And for many students, that was all they did—show the object to the class and stand there smiling. They almost all seemed to love their chance to stand in front of the class, but getting them to speak, especially more than a word or two, was an entirely different matter. Only a few students who were already verbal and outgoing really talked and shared during this activity. I soon realized I wanted the children to gain more from this experience and really learn to share and listen. Since that time, I have used various forms of "daily news" and "weekly news" with students in kindergarten through third grade.

As that first weekly news began to evolve, I was amazed and thrilled with the unlimited opportunities it provided for both teaching and learning experiences. The most dramatic differences came as I began incorporating writing into this time of sharing—and not just writing by me or by the students, but a joint effort to negotiate the text and work together to get it down on paper correctly. Little did I know at that time that I was using interactive writing with my students, providing them with the support and help they needed as they developed and grew into readers and writers. Now I use interactive writing in my classroom every day because it is a powerful tool that actively engages students in purposeful reading, writing, speaking, and listening. Our weekly news is one area that provides an excellent opportunity to use interactive writing strategies to directly teach language arts skills through meaningful, student-generated text.

WHAT IS WEEKLY NEWS?

My students each have the opportunity to share one thing a week that will be put in the weekly news. They share things that are meaningful to them; quite often they share about things they like, their family, their friends, things they do after school or on weekends, or things we do in class. Because students are sharing what is meaningful and relevant to them, a natural outcome is language development for English language learners (ELLs) as well as native English speakers. They hear many words and phrases modeled, and they soon begin using them in their news. After all students have shared and their news has been recorded on chart paper using interactive writing strategies, the news is typed each week (at first by me, and later by students) and copies are sent home for the students to read with their families.

Weekly news utilizes all the levels of writing. I begin by introducing the weekly news through modeled writing, and I incorporate interactive writing as soon as possible as we work our way through the various levels of writing. Modeled writing allows me to demonstrate the skills and ideas I want to emphasize. Shared writing involves the students more as I negotiate text with them and elicit responses from them. Interactive writing, although done to some extent at each level, allows for direct teaching opportunities with each student as we work together on the text. Guided writing provides opportunities for students to broaden their writing skills, working directly with me in small groups. Independent writing enables students to create and write their own text, which they later edit with peers and with me. These levels make up a continuum of teacher scaffolding to be used in writing. Their functions as they relate to our weekly news are shown in Figure 16.

The whole class begins at modeled writing, and as students progress in their literacy and language development, they move through the different levels. This allows for students to work at their own level; therefore, students are challenged, not frustrated. While one student may still need my support in shared writing, another student is progressing through the levels. I provide instruction on an individual basis, while working with the whole class, small groups, or individual students, no matter what their level.

WHY DO I USE WEEKLY NEWS IN MY CLASSROOM?

Through weekly news, students are actively involved in purposeful reading, writing, speaking, listening, and viewing, and in visually representing. When students are involved in all the areas of language arts, there are numerous opportunities for growth and literacy development.

FIGURE 16 Continuum of teacher scaffolding in writing.

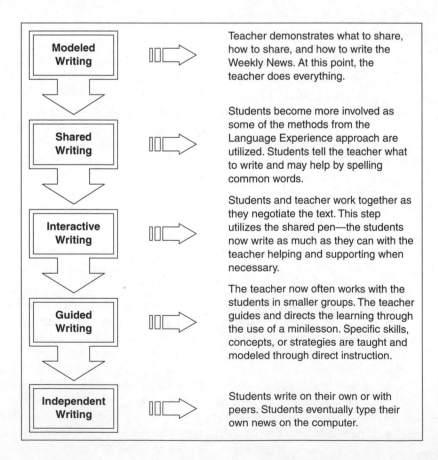

Modeled Writing
Teacher demonstrates what to share, how to share, and how to write the Weekly News. At this point, the teacher does everything.

Shared Writing
Students become more involved as some of the methods from the Language Experience approach are utilized. Students tell the teacher what to write and may help by spelling common words.

Interactive Writing
Students and teacher work together as they negotiate the text. This step utilizes the shared pen—the students now write as much as they can with the teacher helping and supporting when necessary.

Guided Writing
The teacher now often works with the students in smaller groups. The teacher guides and directs the learning through the use of a minilesson. Specific skills, concepts, or strategies are taught and modeled through direct instruction.

Independent Writing
Students write on their own or with peers. Students eventually type their own news on the computer.

Reading. Students begin by reading what they have shared so it is a familiar text. They reread the text several times, which provides opportunities for them to learn directionality of print, spaces between words, basic sight words or common words, the correlation between spoken and written words, and beginning letter sounds. Their early success allows them to be willing to take risks later.

Writing. As students begin the writing phase of weekly news, they again start out successful. They begin by writing their name or maybe even just the first letter of their name. As they gain experience, they start writing the first letter of words or the sounds they hear in words. By using interactive writing, students learn writing skills within the context of what they shared and are familiar with. Students use what they know and then begin to take risks with the things they are learning. I use this time for direct teaching to the individual needs of each student.

Listening. All students have the opportunity to listen as classmates take turns sharing their news. They listen again as I repeat and rephrase the news. They are actively listening because they will need to repeat what they hear. They continue to listen while the news is being written, so they can help supply the word that comes next in the sentence. They are also listening for ideas of things to share in their news.

Speaking. Weekly news provides all students with opportunities to speak and to share, using familiar and comfortable words. This is especially helpful for my ELL students. Because the news is about them, they are eager and willing to share. Often those students learning English begin with brief statements, such as "I play" and "I like my mom." Students are also speaking as they repeat what classmates share. By repeating what other students share and what I have corrected and reworded, they learn new words and phrases. It is amazing how quickly their sentences become longer and more complex.

Viewing. The students have an opportunity to view the weekly news in a variety of ways. First of all, they view the original text as it is written on chart paper or typed on the computer. They also view the news and illustrations of the students in their group as they work on the news during the week. And finally, they view the published newspaper.

Visually Representing. The news that the students write each week is visually represented in the form of our weekly newspaper. The students have the opportunity to give input about some of the things they want in the newspaper. As they progress through the year and learn the necessary skills, they can create their own publication, choosing different fonts, styles, and artwork. They are also able to draw illustrations that go with their weekly news during the week at a literacy center. Once the news is typed on the computer, a student will often choose a graphic or clip art picture to include.

I use weekly news to meet a large number of goals and objectives. It is so versatile that it can be used in a number of ways to produce literacy skills and behaviors in the students. My purposes are always changing and growing to make the most of learning opportunities. For me, weekly news is multifaceted and expandable, allowing for multiple uses and incorporating a variety of skills and learning opportunities.

HOW DOES WEEKLY NEWS USE INTERACTIVE WRITING?

The following steps give an overview of the process for first- and second-grade students. The process is easily adaptable for various grade levels and abilities.

Modeled Writing. I model and demonstrate for the students using various writing and reading strategies. This is also the time to show by example the different types of items to be included in their news. I begin with the whole class. I share a short sentence such as, "Last weekend I went to the mountains." The sentence is then rephrased and I say to the students, "Last weekend Mrs. Schaefer went to the mountains." The students repeat the sentence with me and I then write it for them on chart paper, demonstrating a variety of skills and writing strategies as I go. We read back the finished sentence together.

Shared Writing: Teacher Writes. After a sufficient amount of modeling by me, the students are eager to begin sharing. This is still done whole class. I choose several students a day to share something they would like to have in the weekly news. One student shares; I repeat the sentence, adding the student's name and making necessary changes in sentence structure, and the student now repeats what I said. At this point, I still record the student's news on chart paper while continuing to ask that student what word comes next. After I have finished writing the sentence, the student who shared now reads back his or her news to the class.

Shared Writing: Students Start Writing. I continue with shared writing but include more input from the students as they now write their own names on the chart paper and begin to help with the spelling of common or familiar words. The whole class at this point repeats each student's news and helps to make sure I write every word. When I have finished writing the news, the student who shared will point to each word and read the news to the class. Following this, the whole class reads back the news as the student who shared points to each word.

Interactive Writing. Now I move to a more formal stage of interactive writing. At this point, I sometimes start working with smaller groups, but the whole class still works well. Students supply the news as in the previous steps, but now they write as much as they can with my help when necessary. I use a black pen, and students pick any colored pen they would like. Using the black pen makes it easy for me to later review the students' work for assessment purposes and to plan specific literacy lessons. I follow the interactive writing format as described in Figure 1 on page 3. This is a valuable stage because it allows for innumerable teaching opportunities and builds confidence in the students. Many students remain at this stage for a good part of the year.

Guided Writing. At this point , I still use interactive writing, but the students begin to help each other. I have found it works best to meet with smaller groups as they begin to help each other. I let each student choose a different colored pen, and I still use the black pen. Students each sign their names on the bottom of the paper with the pen they used so I can refer to it later. By using different colors, I am able to quickly tell which students contributed which parts of the sentence. At this level, I am more of an observer, helping and guiding when necessary and making use of those teachable moments.

Independent Writing. Many of the students are now ready to begin independent writing. They still often work in a group and get help from peers but have weaned themselves from me for the most part. My role now is to encourage and facilitate as the students really begin to problem solve and take risks in their writing. I still help with editing and correcting. In the afternoon, the students who wrote news that day read their news to the class and then point to the words while the whole class reads the news back. I have five groups in my class, so each day, one group shares its news. On Friday, students each read their news one more time while I type it on the computer. I add any notes or announcements I have and supply weekly classroom information for parents. I then copy it and it is ready to be sent home on Monday.

Writing Process. Students who are ready now begin using the entire writing process. The students write their news on their own or with peers and revise it. They make necessary changes and additions as they conference with one another. I have them first edit on their own and then with peers before they edit with me. They are required to make corrections and are responsible for having their news typed on the computer by Friday. The students have created something they are excited about and proud of when the newspaper goes home on Monday.

By now, many students are writing short paragraphs and including graphics in the final publication. The process can continue as far as you want to take it. In my classroom, the weekly news process is always changing, growing, and moving from student dependence to independence.

WHAT SHOULD THE PUBLISHED WEEKLY NEWS LOOK LIKE?

I want the product to meet the needs and purposes that I have established for my classroom. Two samples of published weekly news are shown, one from early in the year and the other from the end of the year. By comparing the news, you can see how the students have developed through the year.

Figure 17 is taken from a weekly news several months into the first-grade year. As you can see, the sentences are simple, short, and usually about things the students like. I also use a larger print early in the year. This first sample shows how the front page of each weekly news looks. I use a template with the title and the typed information at the bottom of the page constant. Each week, I fill in the date near the top and the categories at the bottom with the appropriate names.

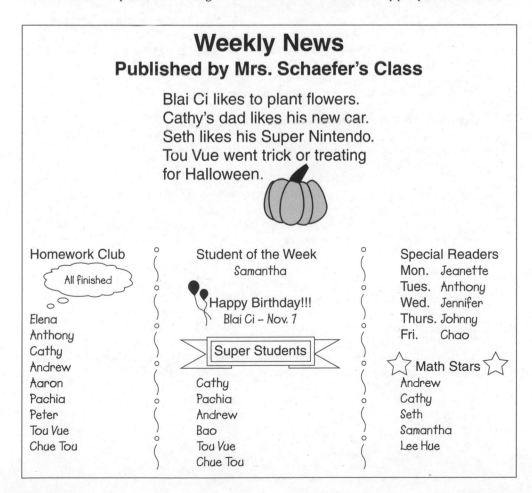

FIGURE 17 Weekly news at the beginning of the year.

The news the students have written is typed and copied on the main portion of the front page. The rest of the news is copied onto the back or additional pages.

Figure 18 is the back page of the weekly news at the end of first grade. For this particular issue, we did not include any illustrations or graphics, but you can easily see the growth in the students' writing over the year. Most students have progressed to writing several, more complex sentences. They are not only writing more, but also reading these longer entries. Even the English language learners and the students in special education programs have shown tremendous growth.

Just as there were goals and objectives to be met while going through the process of creating the weekly news, there are several purposes for publishing the newspaper. My purposes include: providing students with something to read that is relevant and meaningful to them; encouraging students to read at home with their parents and discussing possible topics for future news publications; communicating classroom events and activities to the home; keeping families involved in the child's classroom; informing parents of student progress and achievement; and keeping the principal informed of things happening in class.

I use weekly news in my classroom to help the students:

- make connections between spoken and written words
- develop confidence as writers, readers, speakers, and listeners

FIGURE 18 Weekly news at the end of the school year.

This summer Elena is going to the beach with her family. She is going to swim with her surf board with her dad and her uncle.

For vacation Jeanette is going camping with her dad at the beach. They are going to fish.

At Anthony's dad's house he is going to play baseball. He is going to get a trophy at the pizza place for baseball.

Peter's dad is going to take his family to the park. They will play there and catch fish.

Tou Vue is going to play with his cousins for the summer. He has three cousins.

For vacation Cathy is going to sleep over at her cousin's house. They will play ball and play jump rope. She has fun there.

During the summer Bao is going to play at the park. She will play with her sisters.

This summer Samantha is going to get wet with her new crazy daisy. She got it from Wal Mart. She thinks it will be fun. She will play with it with her friends.

This summer Andrew is going to play with his uncle and his cousin. They are going to watch TV. They are going to watch Free Willy and play sports. Some of Andrew's friends might come over and play with them too. It should be a lot of fun.

Chue Tou will go to the park and eat pizza when we get out of school.

On vacation Seth is going to go to the park with his friend, William. They are going to play on the swings, play tag, play basketball, and climb on the monkey bars.

When we get out of school, Pachia is going to her cousins' house. She is going to play hide-n-seek with them.

On vacation Aaron is going to Disneyland with his auntie and his grandma and his grandpa and someone called Eric. Aaron is going to have fun on Splash Mountain.

- expand their English language development
- build vocabulary and increase the use of high-frequency words
- become problem solvers and take risks
- experience success at their individual levels
- establish a sense of ownership
- incorporate technology into their learning
- make connections between school and home

CONCLUSION

Weekly news has become an indispensable part of my classroom routine. I have found it to be a benefit to my students in developing all the areas of language arts. The interactive writing used throughout this process provides for excellent opportunities to teach to the individual needs of students using a variety of strategies and also allows for continual assessment. This activity grows and develops as the students progress. In addition to the countless skills and concepts it enables me to teach, I enjoy the weekly news because it helps my class each year get to know one another better as we share and talk about the things happening in our lives. What I like best about weekly news is that it allows all students to be successful as they engage in literacy. Not only do I, as a teacher, love the weekly news, but also the students and their parents look forward to the weekly news each Monday. This is truly a rewarding experience that I hope you will make a part of your classroom.

A Picture Is Worth a Thousand Words

Marlis Becker

"Pang, go climb on the bars! Mike, you hang upside down! Look at me and smile," said Joshua.

"Mai, stand under the tree with Amy and Yer. Hug the tree. Look at the camera. Say cheese," said Chrissy.

"Mrs. Becker, can I take your picture with Choua?" asked Pang Lee.

The children were excited and anxious to capture photos of their friends in action. Most of these children had never handled a camera, so this activity was truly a thrill.

I use interactive writing on a daily basis in my classroom, and I'm always looking for new ways to incorporate it into different areas of the curriculum. On this day, the children were photographing each other; we would later write about these pictures using interactive writing.

I teach in a school with a high population of Southeast Asian students. Of the 20 second graders in my class, 15 are Asian and learning English as a second language. These students range from the early production stage to the speech emergence stage of learning English. Because of their various stages of English proficiency, I have found that interactive writing is an invaluable tool in teaching the children to listen, speak, read, and write in English.

I purchase inexpensive disposable cameras for the students to use. I try to have one camera for every five or six children, and they learn they must share. Polaroid cameras can also be used; the advantage to these is that students can immediately see how the photos turn out.

Before going outside to begin the picture-taking session, I spend a lot of time talking about acceptable behavior during this activity. Because of the high level of excitement, we need to establish ground rules before leaving the classroom. We consider the importance of sharing and cooperating with each other, and the need for patience while waiting our turn. We talk about ways we can help each other during our "photo shoot." I also determine the area in which students must remain so I know where they are at all times.

Next, we discuss how to use the camera and what makes a good picture. Children have the opportunity to look through the camera lens and familiarize themselves with what it looks like and how it is used. I point out that what they see in that little square lens is what will appear in their photos. I also remind them to hold the camera still. We talk about the kinds of things students can do to make their photos interesting: how the photo subject should show some action without moving. We want to see clear pictures. We discuss props the children might need to make interesting pictures, such as hats, balls, flowers, and items made in class. For example, we took photos one day after students made pinwheels and floating streamers to check for moving air; they made for great discussion. My goal is to make the photos as action filled as possible so the students have much to talk and write about. The children are usually very creative with their actions and poses for the camera.

With this foundation, we can head outdoors. Now the fun begins! The children are enthusiastic, and it's so much fun to listen as they create photos. They chatter back and forth and they love posing for one another, often begging to have their pictures taken. Even the shy children take part. It is a great way to build self-esteem and teach cooperation.

After the "photo shoot" is complete and all frames have been shot, it is time to have the film developed. If I want to continue the lesson the following day, I take the film to an inexpensive one-hour developer; otherwise, I find the cheapest place in town for developing. If Polaroid film is used, this step is obviously avoided.

When I bring the photos in the following day, the students can hardly wait to see their creations. We look at the pictures one at a time, discussing what we see. I try to get my children to use as much language as possible. This is a great time to talk about describing words (adjectives) and action words (verbs). I encourage the children to use complete sentences. This step often takes enough time that the beginning of writing is better left until the next sitting.

The next time we gather together, I have one or two photos selected to begin our interactive writing activity. We are usually able to write about only one or two photos during one sitting. Because there are many photos, we extend these writing activities over several days or even a week or two. The children are always anxious to see whose picture we will be writing about.

When we begin our writing, I have the children sit on the floor around me. I put the selected picture on an easel beside me. Below the picture, I place an 8 × 11-inch piece of lined or unlined paper. I ask the children to tell me what they see in the photograph. We discuss the picture and decide on one or more sentences describing what is seen. We talk about how many sentences we will write, emphasizing that each sentence is one complete thought. Then we count the words in the first sentence on our fingers, indicating that the space between our fingers is the same as the space between words. We discuss why we need a space between words. We say the first word in the sentence slowly, listening for each sound. Many times, these sounds are unfamiliar to the students because they don't have them in their native language. It takes a lot of practice to become familiar with these sounds. I ask the students if any of them know how to spell the first word. I have a container of colored pens available for the students to use. The volunteer comes up, chooses a pen, and writes the first word. We then read the word and check to see if all the sounds are written by repeating the word slowly. If a correction needs to be made, I cover the error with correction tape and write over it in black pen; I am the only person who uses the black pen. We then say the next word. Students are again asked who can spell that word. We repeat it slowly, listening for sounds. Another student then comes forward to write the word. Again, we reread the entire written text, check for accuracy, and say the next word. We repeat this procedure until the text is complete. If a student makes a mistake, I ask if all the sounds we hear are written. During this writing process, I emphasize correct spelling of words, the use of capital letters, correct punctuation, and plural and past tense endings on words. Another little trick I use to remind them to leave a space between words is a tongue depressor with a little face drawn on the top; this is Mr. Spaceman, and we put him at the end of each word to show that a space is needed before the next word is written. The children tease that Mr. Spaceman will be upset if we don't leave a space for him.

When our writing is completed, we mount the photo and the text on construction paper. Students decorate the paper in various ways using different colors of paper, trimming edges with a decorative scissors or adding stickers and stamps. I encourage students to make the papers as attractive as possible. Then we hang them on the bulletin board. This makes an especially nice display for open house. The children are thrilled to show off their photos to their parents. And the nice thing is that because the children composed the text, they are able to read it! This makes a good impression on parents and also makes the children feel special.

I usually do these activities as a whole group, but they can certainly be easily adapted to a small-group activity. If they are done in small groups, teachers might be able to do more photo descriptions in one day.

I have found that this activity has a high interest level, keeping all students involved. By using interactive writing, the students have made great strides in learning to read, write, and speak English. They have learned to think and to listen to each other. They don't tire of looking at their photos and never seem to run out of ways to describe the scenes, proving once again that a picture is indeed worth a thousand words.

SETTING SAIL ON A SEA OF WORDS: A PASSAGE INTO STORY INNOVATIONS

Diane Leonard

I began creating innovations of children's literature with my first graders a couple of years ago. I would choose a trade book of high interest and appeal, such as *Mary Wore Her Red Dress and Henry Wore His Green Sneakers*, by Merle Peek (1985), and plan a way for my students to respond to it. Initially, my purpose was to engage my young students, most of whom were learning English as a second language, in an extension activity that would connect them back to the book. A natural outgrowth of that was creating innovations of some of our favorite books. Often, our innovations were simple retellings of the story in my students' own words. Occasionally, our innovations went a step beyond the original story and described what might have occurred after the story's original conclusion. Sometimes we created our own conclusions as well. Story innovations became our means of responding to the literature in new and creative ways.

As my students and I worked with retelling the stories, we began to focus on details such as rhyming or plot patterns and created our innovations from them as well. Using the theme and repetitive pattern from *Mary Wore Her Red Dress*, for example, my students and I created our own colorful version entitled "We Wore Our Rainbow Clothes." We included student ideas such as "Xia wore his blue shirt all day long, Nou wore her purple bow all day long, and Jose wore his brown shoes all day long." Everyone contributed a page, and the pages were bound into a class big book to be enjoyed in our library corner.

My purpose in producing literature innovations with my students evolved over time as well. I began to see our innovations as meaningful additions to the environmental print in our classroom. They provided my struggling young readers with additional opportunities to read print that they readily understood and had ownership in. In covering our walls and filling our classroom library with text the children had helped to create, I supported their reading confidence with stories, rhymes, or pattern books that they could not only read and comprehend, but felt pride of ownership in as well.

I frequently taught minilessons on phonics, grammar, and punctuation, as well as process writing skills as students worked on innovation projects. Students also experienced the processes authors use when writing books.

Although I felt my purpose and objectives in completing the various innovation projects were sound, and although my students and I enjoyed creating our literature projects, I became dissatisfied with the overall outcome, because my students were not realizing the growth in reading and writing that I had expected.

They were proud of their work and could read their finished projects, but I wasn't seeing the development in their independent reading and writing skills that I had hoped would transfer over from our class story innovation projects.

I began to realize that I had been neglecting a key component of literacy instruction: Although I was providing ample support for my students through shared and modeled writing experiences, they didn't have enough opportunities to practice what was being demonstrated. Incorporating interactive writing into the innovation process placed more of the responsibility for writing the text into my students' hands. Sharing the pen with them was the missing element I had been searching for to help my students transfer their learning from minilessons and class writing activities into their independent work.

By becoming actively engaged in writing the text for our innovations themselves, using the basic procedure outlined earlier, my students began to develop a deeper sense of ownership about what was written and how it was written. They spent much more time focusing on constructing text for themselves instead of watching me model text writing for them.

I found that interactive writing could provide the support students needed to be successful writers in a very nonthreatening way. They received continual reinforcement in learning about how print works. Because they had so much practice with the actual process of creating words and sentences for themselves as part of interactive writing activities during the day, they became comfortable in trying to read or write new words independently. Writing letters, words, and sentences during interactive writing activities helped students to think out new words they encountered when reading or writing text independently.

I began to notice that students were much more able to read and reread text on their own, even after long periods of time had elapsed since writing projects had been completed. They revisited our innovations more frequently during the day, and enjoyed taking them home to share with their families. Further, they also began to take more risks with their writing and spelling when working on independent assignments.

Interactive writing made its debut as part of the story innovation process in my classroom several years ago, and it proved to be a tremendous success. Over the school year, I developed a procedure that helped my students and me create meaningful innovations of children's literature using interactive writing. The steps are: (1) setting the purpose for the innovation; (2) choosing the book; (3) examining the story structure; (4) considering the length of the original story and its proposed innovation; (5) reading the book; (6) organizing information with the help of graphic organizers; (7) writing the text; and (8) completing the project. Samples from three of the innovations my students and I worked on during the last school year are included to demonstrate the development of students and their story innovations over time.

SETTING THE PURPOSE

Setting the purpose is probably the most important decision to make when beginning a literature innovation, because every other step in the process will be related to the purpose. Setting the purpose can be as simple as providing children with practice using color words, as in my class's innovation of I *Went Walking*, by Sue Williams (1996). Purpose may also include learning how to retell a story, produce a completely different version of the story using the original story's formula or language, or perhaps highlight a key refrain or pattern from the original book to serve as the model for the innovation project.

Children's books are wonderful sources of sophisticated language and wordplay. I use the books' language to point out capitalization, parts of speech, word concepts, and punctuation. Choosing one or two of these language skills as the purpose for the innovation allows students to work with authentic language samples.

Setting the purpose also affects the form the finished project will take, whether a class book, wall story, mural, or quilt. Students enjoy being part of the decision-making process and often have definite ideas about what form their completed innovation should take.

My main purpose in selecting I *Went Walking* was to provide all of my students with the experience of manipulating authentic book language. I wanted them to create their own pages for a class big book that would go into our big book center. Each student would be able to contribute to the project at his or her individual learning level.

My secondary purpose was to provide them with practice reading and using animal names and color words. I chose the repetitive pattern "I saw a (color) (animal) looking at me." from the original book as the pattern for our first innovation attempt.

CHOOSING THE BOOK

After my purpose is set, I choose the story, with one major exception: If, as in the case of I *Went Walking*, I am using a core reading selection from our district's adopted language arts program, the choice has already been made for me before I ever set my purposes. This is an instance where the first step, choosing the book, may be switched with the second step, setting the purpose.

A major consideration for me as a teacher whose students are English Language Learners (ELLs) is that my students often have difficulty understanding stories and book language. For them, innovation projects are helpful because they provide the support for learning English language skills and reading skills students must acquire to develop into successful readers. Innovations allow them to restate ideas and revisit text in familiar language. For students in second grade and above, innovations of the stories in their reading anthologies can help in developing comprehension and language mechanics. They can better understand the core stories while helping to produce an innovation at their individual reading and writing levels.

When choosing a book that is not part of our core reading program, the criteria I use to evaluate a book's suitability for becoming an innovation include the following: student interest, genre, author, structure (rhyming or conventional story patterns), length, and subject matter. I often select books that tie in with the thematic units I am teaching at the time.

Nonfiction books also work well for innovations. For example, if a book about frogs is read as part of a unit on the life cycle of frogs, students might create an innovation using toads, or publish mini research books on different types of frogs that can then be added to the classroom library. Innovations of nonfiction books are also excellent models for students to use as they begin to write their first reports.

It is important that students like the book they are working with because they will revisit the original story and the resulting innovations through related literacy center activities, independent reading, buddy reading, and mini skill and strategy lessons. Offering students a chance to participate in deciding which books to use for innovations helps to keep their interest level high.

EXAMINING THE STRUCTURE

The third step in the innovation process is examining the structure of the book. If it includes rhyming text, particular attention is paid to the rhymes for students to become at ease in trying rhymes of their own. If the book follows conventional story structure, attention will need to be directed to the beginning, middle, and end, especially if it is to be a retelling or the class's own version of the story.

I *Went Walking* is a rhyming book that reveals farm animals a boy encounters as he goes on a walk. The book closely follows the pattern and rhythm of Bill Martin's *Brown Bear, Brown Bear, What Do You See?* (1983). My students had prior experience in kindergarten with that book and its text structure, which made I *Went Walking* a good candidate for our first innovation.

LENGTH

The length of the book is important to consider when creating an innovation. If the original book is very long, children may become mired in comprehension challenges and lose track of the structure while producing their own work, which means it is not a good choice as a model for creating a retelling or alternate version innovation. In that case, perhaps picking out a repetitive theme, refrain, or only a part of the original story might be the wisest course to follow in creating the innovation.

For our own version of I *Went Walking*, I selected the repetitive refrain "I saw a <u>(color)(animal)</u> looking at me." That repetitive pattern was the simplest way to meet the purposes I set in deciding to use the story as a model for our first innovation. The length of the original book was comfortable for student readers: Our 15-page innovation was a big hit with the students as well. Each child author made a page for our I *Went Walking* innovation. In addition, the use of farm animals in the original text tied in neatly with a thematic farm unit my students were working on at the time.

READING THE BOOK

The book chosen for an innovation is generally read in several ways over 3 to 4 days before beginning the innovation. We begin on Monday with the first shared reading, during which the emphasis is on enjoying the author's work. The class sits on the carpet while we find the title, the author, and the illustrator on the front cover. We examine both front and back covers and the title page to make initial predictions about the story inside. We picture walk through the book, noting details such as characters and setting, and making predictions about the story. We then check our predictions during the initial reading.

During the next 3 days or so, we revisit the book with several objectives in mind. In the beginning of the year, we worked on developing concepts about print by looking at the front and back of the book, noting where print began, looking at the return sweep of print, identifying directionality, and framing a letter or word. As the year progressed, I began scanning the books for additional teaching points, such as punctuation, capitalization, consonant digraphs, compound words, rhyming words, contractions, nouns, verbs, and adjectives that could be taught in minilessons during subsequent shared readings of the book. Shared readings usually lasted 15 to 20 minutes, followed by guided reading time with students working in groups with small copies of the big book for about 20 minutes each day. Additional skills lessons took place during guided reading sessions.

Fridays were reserved for our literature innovations. We didn't produce an innovation with every book we read or even every week because I didn't want to burn the children out with too much of a good thing. I tended to alternate literature innovations with other extension activities. Our early innovations, like I *Went Walking*, were easily completed in an hour and a half. Our more recent innovations have taken several days to complete.

| I saw a | b r o w n | h o r s e | looking at me. |
| I saw a | b l u e | b i r d | looking at me. |

FIGURE 19 Pocket chart sentence frames from *I went walking* story innovation.

ORGANIZING THE INFORMATION

Before we began to write an innovation, we generally used some type of graphic organizer to help us develop story comprehension and format. The type of organizer I chose varied from story to story; we have used T-graphs, cyclical charts, Venn diagrams, and story maps or clusters. Students also had a great deal of practice manipulating text in pocket charts. Key text was written on sentence strips in cloze form and on word cards, as seen in Figure 19. Students could change the original text by removing parts of the sentence strips and replacing them with their ideas. Before beginning an innovation, it is important that students—especially those who are struggling with reading or language—gain plenty of experience with the format, sentence structure, and vocabulary of the story through graphic organizer activities.

By Friday of the week that we made our innovation of I *Went Walking*, the students had been given abundant practice with color words, farm animal names, and reenacting the story through dramatic play. I began the innovation lesson with a final reading of the big book. Whenever I got to the refrain, "I saw a (color)(animal) looking at me," I asked the children to clap along. We were paying particular attention to that refrain because we would be using it as the model from which to construct our innovation.

Next, we worked with a pocket chart and sentence strips. I wrote "I saw a ____ ____ looking at me." on sentence strips and placed them in a pocket chart, as shown in Figure 19. I provided extra blank cards for students to fill in using interactive writing to place over the blanks in the sentence frame in the pocket chart.

WRITING THE TEXT

Children took turns, one child per word, writing color words and animal names on cards to fill in the blanks in the sentence frame. I wrote "letter lines" as needed for students. At the beginning of the year, when we were working on this innovation, every child in my room needed the additional support of my adding letter lines during interactive writing activities. As children generated text for the cloze sentence in the pocket chart for I *Went Walking*, I supported their writing by drawing one letter line for each letter in each word they were trying to spell. The sentence frame in the pocket chart read, "I saw a (color)(animal) looking at me."A completed sentence in the pocket chart looked like this:

"I saw a ____ ____ looking at me."

A child chose *blue* as the color word. I wrote: ____ on the blank word card.

Each letter of the word *blue* was represented by a line. We said the word *blue* again and counted the number of letters we needed to spell the word. Then, the word *blue* was written from left to right, with the child using a colored marker to write in the letters she knew. After she added each letter, we repeated the word, stretching it out to help her listen for letter sounds in *blue*. Using a black marker, I wrote in the letters she couldn't hear or didn't know were in the word. Each time we added a letter, we repeated the word. We used correction tape to change mistakes.

The finished word card looked like this: b l u e

I repeated the process for the animal name cards. Each time we completed the color and animal name cards, we placed them in the sentence frame in the pocket chart, and the class practiced reading them together.

During the year, students quickly caught on that if there was a letter line left over after the last letter sound they heard in the word being written, the line must contain silent *e*. Students began taking delight in their cleverness each time they figured out a silent *e* word.

Letter lines provided anchor points for students, allowing them to see the approximate length of the word and the number of letters they needed to be thinking about and listening for as they wrote words.

Although most students seemed to be comfortable writing individual words in the conventional left-to-right sequence, some students tended to focus on the beginning and ending sounds of words as their two anchor points. Once they'd written the initial and final letters of the word they were trying to write, they'd go back and fill in the medial letters. This strategy seemed to give them the support they needed. I accepted either left-to-right sequence or beginning/ending sound strategies from my students.

I observed that as soon as students became more confident writers, they made a natural shift toward the conventional left-to-right spelling sequence used by their peers. I continued to model the left-to-right spelling sequence in all our group activities, but I supported the students using the initial and final anchor point strategy by using it with them on an individual basis until they began to shift over to left-to-right spelling convention.

As the year progressed, students learned that some sounds are represented by two or more letters. During group interactive writing activities, I often asked students to circle these blended sounds to reinforce the understanding that although they may occupy multiple letter lines, the letters are working together to create one sound. The circle around the letters emphasizes this point.

Gradually, as they move along in their spelling and writing development, students need less support from letter lines, until the lines are no longer needed. I write letter lines only as needed to scaffold a child's writing. Near the end of the school year, my students began to ask me not to write the letter lines for them. They were very confident about attempting to spell new words on their own.

I was fascinated during the year to see that students would come to me, my aide, or other students for spelling help on other written work and would often have written letter lines themselves for the sounds they could hear in the words they were trying to spell. I noticed letter lines began to appear frequently in their journals as well. The lines became a powerful tool not only for me to scaffold their learning, but for the students to take responsibility for their own learning as well.

In writing the text for our I *Went Walking* innovation, the children took turns writing color words and animal names as long as their interest was high. We practiced reading the completed sentence frame each time the two blanks were filled in with the word cards the children and I wrote. My writing was always in black marker so that I could see at a glance which letter sounds they needed my help with.

Following the pocket chart lesson, the children watercolor painted the farm animal that they wanted to write about. I provided computer-printed sentence frames of the same frame we had used in the pocket chart to be glued to each child's artwork. I called students one at a time to come fill in the blanks on a sentence frame that was glued onto their artwork. We interactively wrote one-on-one, with me again using a black marker so that I could tell which letters each child needed help writing.

FIGURE 20 Sample student page from *I Went Walking* story innovation.

COMPLETING THE PROJECT

I made a cover for our class book and the first page, which read: "I went walking." "What did you see?" Each succeeding page was student authored and illustrated, as the sample page shown in Figure 20 demonstrates.

We celebrated the completion of the innovation by reading it together and by sharing it with other classes. It was laminated and became the beginning of our class big book center. It quickly became the most popular book in the classroom because everyone could read it. We revisited our book throughout the year to celebrate student writing growth. Students were very proud of their progress when they looked at that first book.

After we had completed and celebrated two or three innovations, Lucy, one of my students who was struggling with reading, came to school with a book that she had written at home. The book had several small sheets of paper haphazardly taped together, with the text written from the back of the book to the front. We had recently completed an innovation story quilt of the book *Rain*, by Robert Kalan (1978). The pattern of the book is simple: "Rain on the (color)(noun)." Ours was entitled *Sun*, and students again filled in the blanks of a cloze sentence. Lucy had written her own *Sun* book. The only words she had spelled correctly were *sun* and some of the color words, but she proudly read it flawlessly to me. We immediately published it on the computer and added it to our class library. Most of the other students in class have followed Lucy's lead and have subsequently written their own book innovations for publication as well.

Lucy continued to show great interest in writing her own books throughout the school year. Occasionally, she would write her own innovation of a favorite book, but as her reading and writing skills improved, she became comfortable writing her own stories. By the end of the year, she was near the top of the class in reading ability.

GROWING WITH INNOVATIONS

As the year progressed and my students became more familiar with book language and sentence structure, we began to experiment a little with our innovations: We learned how to make our own version of a story using the original story's structure

FIGURE 21 Student pages from alternate version of *The Good Bad Cat*.

and format. We published *The Good Bad Dragon* as our innovation of *The Good Bad Cat*, by Nancy Antle (1997). Students had to be very familiar with the sequence of events and vocabulary from *The Good Bad Cat* to be successful writing our alternate version, as illustrated in Figure 21.

For our final innovation of the year, I decided to spend a week with Laura Numeroff's *If You Give a Mouse a Cookie* (1985), a deliciously circular tale of a demanding mouse and an overobliging boy. My children quickly caught on to the pattern of the book: Each time the boy in the story gives the mouse something he wants, the mouse wants something else, until the story ends the same way it begins, with the boy giving the mouse a cookie.

I selected the book with several purposes in mind. It had high student appeal, so I knew my students would enjoy working with the story. It provided the opportunity to teach minilessons on nouns and verbs. It also served as meaningful English language development lessons for my ELL students by building vocabulary about household items. This innovation was also going to give my students a chance to work with a much more complex story; the circular plot line was a sophisticated one for my students to follow. *If You Give a Mouse a Cookie* was our culminating innovation for the year.

Because I thought the concept of giving an animal one thing that might lead to it wanting another might be difficult for my class, I spent much more time building background with this story than with any other. We spent several days looking at cumulative stories, such as *The House That Jack Built* (Adams, 1977) and *There Was an Old Lady Who Swallowed a Fly* (Adams,1973).

FIGURE 22 Cyclical graphic organizer from *If You Give a Mouse a Cookie.*

Just before beginning *If You Give a Mouse a Cookie* with my class, I had my bilingual aide preview the book in Hmong language with the majority of my students. I developed vocabulary with them by bringing real samples of items listed in the story to class. The students and I practiced retelling the story with these real props. We made finger puppets and story props for them to practice with at home or with each other. I placed a copy of the book and a tape at our listening center. I also placed a copy of the book, a storytelling apron, and velcro props at our dramatic play center.

We practiced in the pocket chart with "You can give a (animal) a (item)." This time, the children wrote all the words for the sentence frame interactively on sentence strips as well as filling in the blanks. The children wrote and illustrated their own pages for a class book using this frame. The completed sentence strip frame and word cards stayed in the pocket chart for use as a literacy center activity.

We then used interactive writing to develop a cyclical chart (Bromley, Irwin-De Vitis, & Modlo, 1995) that displayed the order in which story items appeared and labeled them as vocabulary words, as shown in Figure 22. Creating the chart helped students keep track of the story sequence by allowing them to see that providing one item for the mouse in the story led to having to provide another related item. By then, students were able to write independently: "If you give a(n) (animal) a (item), he will want a (related item)".

The completed student pages became a story quilt that students enjoyed rereading as they read around the room. Had my students been a little older or more fluent in English, I probably would have had the class create a completely new version of the book. My students were all very pleased with our class big book and innovation quilt projects.

We subsequently read and enjoyed Laura Numeroff's other books, *If You Give a Moose a Muffin* (1991) and *If You Give a Pig a Pancake* (1998). Students were delighted to see that both of these books follow the same pattern as *If You Give a Mouse a Cookie*. As we were picture walking through *If You Give a Pig a Pancake*, Joe, who had really struggled all year with reading, excitedly interrupted the picture walk to say, "I know why you make us do this. It's so we can put in our heads the words we need so we can read the story." It was one of those "AHA!" moments we all live for as teachers. I praised his discovery, and we enjoyed the story together.

I am convinced that having just used interactive writing to complete the cyclical word bank and the story sequence chart for *If You Give a Mouse a Cookie* helped Joe make that crucial discovery. We had spent all year plugging away at story prediction with Joe. He had thoroughly enjoyed *If You give a Mouse a Cookie* and escorted any visitor to our classroom to our chart where he would retell the original story. He had been very involved in labeling our cyclical word bank and labeling story props using interactive writing. It took a year's worth of experiences and the activities from our latest innovation to help him connect picture walking and prediction to reading print.

Using interactive writing in conjunction with story innovations has been tremendously rewarding for my students. Creating innovations while sharing the pen with my students served as a springboard for them toward independent authorship. The effect on my students' reading comprehension and writing development far exceeded my expectations when I set out to make innovations using interactive writing and children's literature.

REFERENCES

Adams, P. (1973). *There was an old lady who swallowed a fly*. Singapore: Child's Play.

Adams, P. (1977). *The house that Jack built*. Singapore: Child's Play.

Antle, N. (1997). *The good bad cat*. New York: Macmillan/McGraw-Hill.

Bromley, K., Irwin-De Vitis, L., & Modlo, M. (1995). *Graphic organizers*. New York: Scholastic.

Kalan, R. (1978). *Rain*. New York: William Morrow.

Martin, B. (1983). *Brown bear, brown bear, what do you see*? New York: Holt, Rinehart and Winston.

Numeroff, L. (1985). *If you give a mouse a cookie*. New York: Harper & Row.

Numeroff, L. (1991). *If you give a moose a muffin*. New York: Harper & Row.

Numeroff, L. (1998). *If you give a pig a pancake*. New York: Harper & Row.

Peek, M. (1985). *Mary wore her red dress, and Harry wore his green sneakers*. New York: Clarion.

Williams, S. (1996). *I went walking*. San Diego: Harcourt Brace.

WORKING YOUR WAY THROUGH A STORY: BEGINNING, MIDDLE, AND END

Marlis Becker

The *Very Hungry Caterpillar*, by Eric Carle (1969), is a favorite book in my class. When the caterpillar turns into a beautiful butterfly, my students ooh and ahh. It never fails. My students tell me they love the ending because it is "happy" and "pretty." They can easily identify what happens at the end of this story. But what about the beginning and the middle?

It is important for students to learn the parts of a story. They need to know the sequence of events in order to comprehend and accurately retell the story. Otherwise, they will not become confident, fluent, and accurate readers. One of the ways I help my students develop good comprehension skills is to teach the three parts of story structure: beginning, middle, and end. *The Very Hungry Caterpillar* is a perfect story to use for this activity because the three parts are easy for the students to see. Because I use interactive writing daily in my classroom, I have learned it is an effective way to teach the parts of stories.

I teach in a school with a large population of nonnative English speakers. Of the 20 students in my second-grade classroom, 15 are Southeast Asian and are learning English as a second language. These students range from the early production stage, using just a few words to express themselves, to the speech emergence stage of learning English, where they are using simple phrases and sentences. Even two of my native English students have very limited vocabularies. Because of these varying stages, interactive writing is an invaluable tool to support students' English language development.

I prefer to work with a story over a period of several days. The first day is spent reading and discussing. The following days, we do the interactive writing and the artwork, one part each day. It usually helps students' understanding if the entire lesson is not done all at one time. They need time to develop their understanding in order to fully comprehend the story. Also, when doing interactive writing, I have found that my students cannot concentrate on intensive English tasks for much more than 30 minutes. For younger students, the time might be even shorter.

After selecting a story, I read it to the students. We discuss what we have read, and I have them retell the story to me with as much detail as they can recall. We analyze the story, talking about the characters and the setting. This is followed by a discussion of what happened in the beginning, middle, and end. I remind them that in the beginning, we learn about the characters in the story, who they are, and what they do. In the beginning, we also discover the setting of the story, and the beginning of a problem is revealed. From this, we move on to a discussion of what happens in the middle of the story. Here we learn that the problem actually begins and continues to build. New characters may appear. There may be interaction between the characters, and they may face difficulties in dealing with the problem. We realize that the middle of the story is the longest part because that is when most of the action and interaction between characters takes place. In the end of the story, the problem is solved, and this is usually the most obvious part of the story to students. With this discussion completed, we stop for the day. Because of the length of time involved in the initial reading and discussion, I do not begin the interactive writing process at this time.

On the following day, we begin writing. With the children sitting on the floor around me, we reread the story and review what happened in the beginning, middle, and end. Today we write only about the beginning. We decide what happened in the beginning and work together to form sentences, emphasizing that each sentence is a complete thought. When writing about *The Very Hungry Caterpillar*, for example, the children decided on, "A little caterpillar popped out of an egg. He was very hungry." We begin with the first sentence by counting each word on our fingers, indicating that the space between our fingers is the same as the space between the words. We discuss why we need a space between words. We say the first word in the sentence slowly, listening for each sound. Many times these sounds are unfamiliar to the students because they don't have them in their native language. I ask if anyone knows how to spell the first word. I have a container of colored pens available for students to use. A volunteer comes up, chooses a pen, and writes the first word. Together we then read the word and check to see if all the sounds are written by repeating the word slowly. If an error is made, I cover it with correction tape and write over it in black pen; I am the only person who uses the black pen. Then we say the next word. I ask again who can spell the word. We repeat it slowly, listening for sounds. Another student comes forward to write the word. Again, we reread the entire written text, check for accuracy, and say the next word. We repeat this procedure until the text is complete. During this writing process, I emphasize correct spelling of words, the use of capital letters, correct punctuation, and plural and past tense endings on words. I use a tongue depressor with a face drawn on the top to remind them to leave a space between words. I call him Mr. Spaceman, and we put him at the end of each written word to show that a space is needed before the next word is written. When we have completed the sentences about the beginning, the lesson is brought to closure for the day.

The following day, we review what we did previously. We once again read the book and what we wrote for our beginning. We then decide what to write about the middle of the book. We recall that this section will be the longest because this is where all the action takes place. We follow the same procedure and write our sentences on a different piece of paper. Because the middle is the longest part of the book, the students will have more to write about. If the text requires more illustrations than will fit on the paper on which it will be mounted, use a separate piece of paper to write sentences. I can then mount the middle part on two or more sections as needed. For the middle, my students write, "Every day the caterpillar ate through lots and lots of food. He got a stomach ache. He ate through a green leaf and felt better. Now he was very big. He built a cocoon." I put the first two sentences and illustrations on one section and the last three sentences and illustrations on another. On the fourth day, we continued the activity by repeating the steps as we decide on and write about the ending of the story. This is the part the children love. Now they write, "He came out of the cocoon. He was a beautiful butterfly!"

With all the writing completed, we move on to illustrating. Because we need fewer illustrations than there are students in the class, students work in pairs or small groups to make the pictures for each of the three sections. Or perhaps a few students can be chosen to do the work. The first and last sections may need only one or two illustrations, whereas the middle usually requires several. After the

FIGURE 23 Bulletin board illustrating the parts of a story.

illustrations are finished, I then mount the written text with the corresponding illustrations on a round sheet of butcher paper. The beginning section is put on a green circle, the middle sections are put on yellow circles, and the end section is put on a red circle. I then put the circles in order on the bulletin board to form a caterpillar, as shown in Figure 23. The size of the papers for written text and illustrations should be adjusted to a convenient size depending on how much bulletin board space is available. I do not always mount the story on a caterpillar shape, but in the case of *The Very Hungry Caterpillar*, it seems appropriate. For other stories, I might create a different shape or use a simple square or rectangular piece of paper. But I always use the same three colors in the same order; the color and order symbolize the beginning, the middle, and the end of the story for my students. If I want a different format, I sometimes make this into a large class book for the students to read in our class library. Another adaptation is to make individual booklets with the text for students to read and illustrate.

This lesson could be done with the whole class or a small group. If the story requires only a few illustrations, it may simplify matters to do the lesson with fewer children so that all can participate in making the illustrations. I prefer to stretch the activities out over a week, but teachers can certainly modify the procedure to suit their particular students' needs.

This activity has helped my students tremendously in building their comprehension skills. It has helped them to understand that stories must have a beginning, a middle, and an end. The students show me that they have learned this concept through their own writings. And again, through interactive writing, the students are learning from their peers as they work together, broadening their abilities in learning to think, listen, read, write, and speak English.

REFERENCE

Carle, Eric. (1969). *The very hungry caterpillar.* Cleveland: Collins-World.

Teaching Skills and Strategies Through Interactive Writing

Theresa Kasner

Classroom language arts instruction should provide students with both skills and strategies to help them develop into fluent readers and writers. One of the best ways I have found to teach skills and strategies is through interactive writing. It is a powerful tool that actively involves students during literacy lessons and provides explicit demonstrations of how language works through teacher support and guidance. According to Vygotsky (1978), "What a child can do with assistance today she will be able to do by herself tomorrow" (p. 78).

Strategies are problem-solving methods and behaviors that both readers and writers use. Clay (1991) describes strategies as operations that allow readers and writers to apply, transform, relate, reproduce, and interpret information for communication. Through teacher scaffolding, students learn many strategies that help them to become successful readers and writers, such as how to reread text, make personal connections with text, and monitor their own reading and writing.

Readers and writers use skills, on the other hand, to process information. Skill use will eventually become automatic, and students will instinctively use skills as they read and write. There are five types of skills that students learn to help them read and write fluently: meaning-making skills, decoding and spelling skills, study skills, language skills, and reference skills (Tompkins, 2002). Some examples of skills are capitalization, punctuation, spelling rules, letter formation, spacing between words, possessives, and syllabication.

In this chapter, I share a few of the interactive writing lessons I use to teach skills and strategies in my second-grade classroom. I have found that when students are actively engaged in the process of learning skills and strategies through meaningful lessons, they are more likely to apply this new knowledge to their own reading and writing.

A STRATEGY LESSON: PREDICTING

During a Directed Listening and Thinking Activity (DLTA), developed by Russell Stauffer (1975), students make predictions about a specific story and then stop at different points in the story to confirm or reject their predictions. The students learn to actively listen for the information that would confirm their prediction.

DLTA is divided into three steps: Preparing to Read, Reading Aloud, and Reflecting on Predictions. I use interactive writing during the first two stages of a

DLTA lesson, and the third step is conducted as whole-group/class discussion and reflection or as a literature journal activity.

The lesson begins with the students looking at the cover of the book that I will be reading to them. First, I read the title of the book and I ask them to think quietly about what the book might be about. I stress the importance of keeping their predictions to themselves, so they don't rob other students of their own thinking. Next, I ask students to share their predictions, which they must back up with a reason. For example, when I read the class the story *Matthew's Dream*, by Leo Lionni (1991), one student predicted that it was going to be about a mouse eating cheese. There is a mouse on the cover, but no cheese to be found. When I asked what made him think of cheese, the student replied, "Mice love cheese!"

Once a student makes a prediction and can back it up with supporting information, the class adds it to the DLTA story chart. Working together, we negotiate a sentence and count the number of words on our fingers. Next, the students take turns coming up to write the sentence on the chart, one word at a time. Each word is stretched out slowly as we all listen for the individual phonemes that make up the word. After each word is written, the complete sentence is reread and the pen is passed to the next student to continue the steps. While this process proceeds, students are writing the sentence in their own literature journals. Figure 24 shows the predictions the students made before we read *Matthew's Dream*. The number of predictions that are placed on the chart depends on the individual students and how long they can focus.

After this step, the students are ready to hear the story, eagerly listening for the class predictions. I stop from time to time and we discuss any of the predictions that have been proved or disproved, putting a star by those that have been proved. Sometimes new predictions are added at this stage, following the same procedure of negotiating a sentence and having children come up to add the words to the chart, stretching out each word to listen for the letter sounds.

When the story is finished, we again place a star next to the predictions that have been proved. After rereading all the predictions that were confirmed, the students select one prediction and write specific information from the story that supported that prediction in their journals.

It is important to remember that DLTA works only with books that students are unfamiliar with. If a child has heard the story before, I encourage him or her to keep this knowledge of the book a secret so that we can see what predictions the other students come up with.

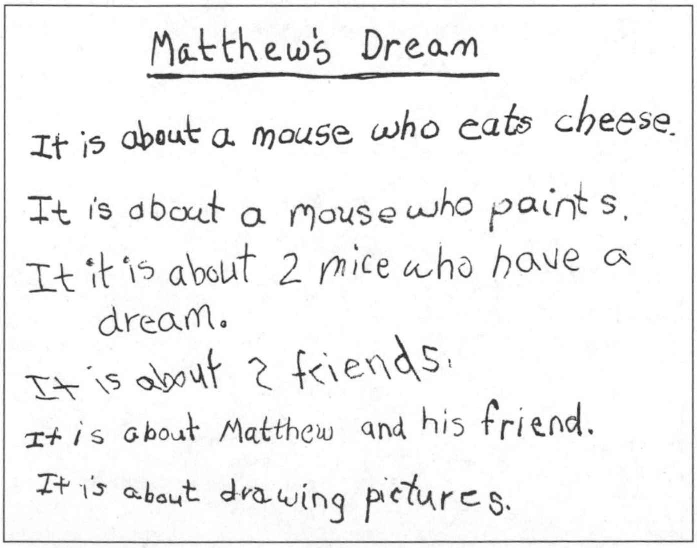

FIGURE 24 Student predictions from *Matthew's Dream*.

> Matthew's Dream
>
> It is about a mouse who eats cheese.
>
> It is about a mouse who paints.
>
> It it is about 2 mice who have a dream.
>
> It is about 2 friends.
>
> It is about Matthew and his friend.
>
> It is about drawing pictures.

A MINILESSON: ADJECTIVES

Interactive writing is an excellent way to actively involve students during the teaching of minilessons. One particular lesson I taught revolved around the story *Hairs*, by Sandra Cisneros (1994): I wanted to teach the students about adjectives and how they help to paint a clear picture for the reader.

I began by reviewing the definition of adjectives. I had some adjectives written out on cards that we read and talked about. I asked the students if they noticed anything about these words, if they had anything in common. I told them that these words are called adjectives; they are words that describe something. We talked about how they are different from nouns. Next, in small groups, the students took turns sorting a stack of cards that contained nouns and adjectives.

Next, I shared the story *Hairs* with the students. I asked them to listen for the adjectives the author used to describe the hair of the different members of her family. After the story was finished, we discussed the adjectives used and decided that they could be divided into different categories, such as texture, style, color, and smell. I made a chart, and we added the adjectives the author used to it. Next, I asked students to look at my hair and come up with more adjectives to add to our chart, as seen in Figure 25. Each word was stretched out slowly as we listened to the individual phonemes. Every student wrote one word on the chart, placing it into the proper category. If a student made a mistake during this process, we used the 1-inch-wide whiteout tape, which I refer to as "boo-boo tape," to cover up the error. Then the child rewrote the correct letters, which means that spelling skills are authentically reinforced. During this whole-group time, the students wrote all the words into their journals, putting each word into its proper category. We continued with this process until every child had a chance to write a word on the chart.

The next day, we revisited the story and reread the list of adjectives. As a class, we wrote a descriptive piece about my hair, using the adjectives to make the piece more descriptive. When a sentence was generated, we counted out the words and began the process of writing it interactively. Each word was stretched out while we listened to individual phonemes. I pulled student names from my name jar, and the students chosen took turns writing a sentence. As each new word was written, we reviewed the sentence until it was completed. We continued this process until we had a clear description of my hair, as shown in Figure 26.

Next, I divided the class into pairs, and they wrote a short description of their partner's hair. We got into small groups to listen to each piece, asking questions and discussing adjectives that could be added to make the piece more clear. If there were new adjectives they wanted to add, the students wrote them on the chart.

FIGURE 25 Student-generated list of adjectives for hair.

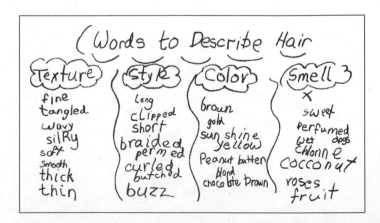

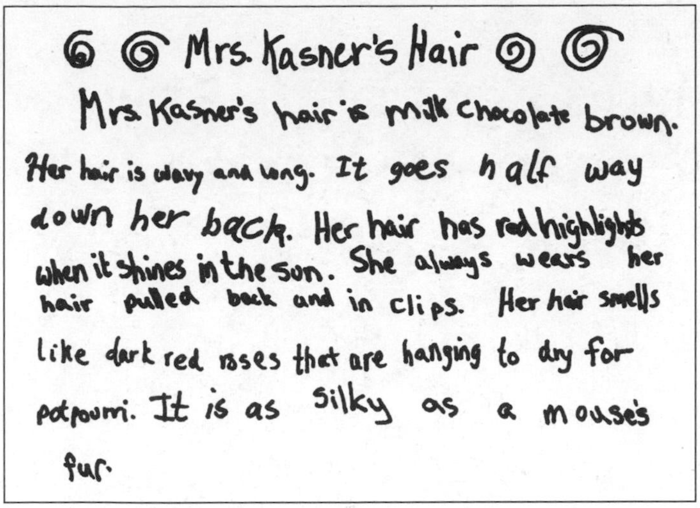
Mrs. Kasner's Hair

Mrs. Kasner's hair is milk chocolate brown. Her hair is wavy and long. It goes half way down her back. Her hair has red highlights when it shines in the son. She always wears her hair pulled back and in clips. Her hair smells like dark red roses that are hanging to dry for potpourri. It is as silky as a mouse's fur.

FIGURE 26 Students' descriptive writing about hair.

The final product of this series of lessons was a written description, filled with vivid adjectives, of their family members' hair.

CONCLUSION

I have found interactive writing to be a wonderful tool to use when teaching skills and strategies. It is a way to scaffold the learning experience while providing varying levels of support for individual children depending on their abilities. It is a method for engaging children in a level of writing that would otherwise be considered too difficult for many of them, yet with a great deal of success for all.

REFERENCES

Cisneros, S. (1994). *Hairs*. New York: Random House.

Clay, M. (1991). *Becoming literate: The construction of inner control*. New York: Heinemann.

Lionni, L. (1991). *Matthew's dream*. New York: Random House.

Stauffer, R. G. (1975). *Directing the reading-thinking process*. New York: Harper & Row.

Tompkins, G. (2002). *Language arts: Content and teaching strategies* (5th ed.). Upper Saddle River, NJ: Merrill/Prentice Hall.

Vygotsky, L. S. (1978). *Mind in society: The development of higher psychological processes*. Cambridge, MA: Harvard University Press.

Powering the Poet's Pen: Writing Poetry Interactively

Kimberly Clark

Children love the rhyme and rhythm of poetry: the way the words sound as they roll off their teachers' tongues, and the way the words tickle their own tongues, as they chant poems. Imaginative and poetic simply by nature, children can be successful poets. With the support of interactive writing, children of all ages and language backgrounds can begin their journey toward independent poetry writing.

Writing poetry interactively follows the same basic steps as other interactive writing lessons. There are just a few differences: Normally the text is negotiated on a sentence-by-sentence basis, but with poetry, the text is agreed upon line by line. After a line is completed, the entire text is reread to check that it sounds right and feels right in the students' mouths. The five steps to writing a poem interactively are:

1. Choose grouping type (whole class, small group).
2. Choose paper (sentence strips, chart paper).
3. Choose type of poem (formula, model).
4. Write the poem interactively.
5. Illustrate and publish the poem.

The first step in writing a poem interactively is deciding how to group the students. An interactive lesson can be done with the whole class or in small groups; this decision depends on the needs of the students and teacher preference. If the teacher's focus is on a skill all students need (or if the teacher wants more discussion and student involvement), whole-group work is best. On the other hand, small groups are in order if the teacher is working on a skill or concept that just a few children need, or if a group needs more teacher support. A great deal of oral language and English language development occurs during an interactive writing lesson. This may help determine the grouping of the students.

In the second step, the teacher decides which type of paper to use for the writing. Both sentence strips and chart paper work well. An advantage to sentence strips is that they can be used for center activities, because children can sequence and illustrate the poem.

Next, the teacher decides which type of poem is going to be written. All types of poems can be written interactively, but I have found the two most suitable types for primary children are model poems and formula poems.

The fourth step is the actual interactive writing of the poem. The fifth and final step is illustrating and publishing the text. Students enjoy illustrating the lines that they have written, and the text can either be displayed on the wall or become a class book.

Following are several examples of this process. The first uses a model poem, and the others use formula poems.

MODEL POEMS

Model poems provide children with an adult model that they can use as a skeleton for their own writing. Children should be familiar with the model poem and enjoy reading it before using it as a model for their own writing.

Many poems that children enjoy contain rhyming words. If the model poem has rhyming words, then it is important that the students recognize where in the poem the rhymes occur. This knowledge will help them during their text negotiation, because they will need to develop a list of possible rhymes on a separate piece of paper. As each line is read and agreed upon, the students share the pen with the teacher and write as much of the text as they are able to write. If a line does not sound or feel right, then the students make changes in the text; they may add, delete, or change a word. The students know how the rhyme and rhythm of the poem should sound and feel because their poem is based on a very familiar model. If a question arises, the model poem is reread.

A good example of a model poem is Jack Prelutsky's "I Did Not Eat Your Ice Cream" (Prelutsky, 1990), a poem about the things the author did not do. Each line follows the format "I did not . . . ." A first/second-grade class rewrote Prelutsky's poem as follows:

I Did Not Eat Your Pizza
I *did not eat your pizza,*
I *did not grab your toys,*
I *did not leave (your) Spider Man,*
Outside with (all) the boys.

I *did not hide your* <u>turtle</u>,
I *did not steal your bike,*
It must have been my brother,
We look a lot alike.

This poem was written by the whole class on chart paper, and a great deal of discussion and revising took place as the children negotiated the text. The words in parentheses were not originally part of the text but were added through negotiation. The underlined word <u>turtle</u> was also a subject of great debate: Many of the students wanted a shorter word, such as *dog* or *cat*, but they decided by looking at the model poem that the author's original word, *sweater*, was a much longer word. His word required two claps because it had two syllables, so they agreed that their word should have the same. The students then developed a list of two-syllable words, and the word *turtle* was finally agreed upon.

On the lines that were the most difficult to write, the children relied very heavily on Prelutsky's poem, and changed only one or two words. Nevertheless, upon the completion of this poem, they felt great ownership.

The children made a class book by writing and illustrating the pages. These were then laminated, and the book was bound and placed in the class library for everyone to enjoy.

FORMULA POEMS

Probably the easiest type of poem for young children to write is the formula poem. Instead of using rhyme, as more traditional poems do, formula poems begin each line the same way or have a particular kind of word in every line (Tompkins, 2002). The formula provides a strong structure for the children to follow but still allows for individual creativity. A few examples of formula poems are "Color" poems, "I Wish . . . " poems, and "Five Senses" poems.

The formula for "Color" poems is that each line of the poem begins with a color word. The color can change in each line, or one color can be used throughout. If more details are added, the lines can be expanded into stanzas (Koch, 1980).

A group of first-grade students wrote a "Color" poem about the color green with two-line stanzas; they began each stanza with "Green is. . . ." Their final poem reads as follows:

Green is a turtle
crawling in the grass.

Green is a leprechaun
hiding all his gold.

Green is a dragon
blowing fire from his mouth.

Green is a frog
hopping on a lily.

Green is a soft grape
mushy in my mouth.

Children began this poetry-writing activity as a whole class by brainstorming a list of all green things they could think of. As each item was mentioned, we wrote it interactively on a piece of chart paper. Part of their class homework that evening was to look for other interesting green items around their homes and neighborhoods. The next morning, the original list was reread, and the new items were added. The "favorite five" green things were then chosen to become part of the class poem.

The teacher met with the children in small groups to write the poem interactively on sentence strips. Each group chose one of the green things and negotiated the text for that particular stanza of the poem. All ideas were considered, and a great deal of debate and discussion occurred during this small-group writing.

After the class completed the poem, the sentence strips were put in a pocket chart to be sequenced during center activities. The class soon realized that they could construct some very funny poems by mixing up the second lines to each stanza. The children then worked in pairs to publish their poem, and they rewrote and illustrated the text for a class big book.

When writing "I Wish" poems, children begin each line of their poem with the words "I wish" and complete each line with a wish (Koch, 1980). Once the "wish" lines have been completed, the ideas can be expanded into a full "I Wish" poem.

A class of first-grade students wrote a class collaboration. Part of their poem reads as follows:

I wish I had a monster truck.
I wish I had a whole bunch of toys.
I wish I had a remote control car.
I wish I was a bunny.
I wish I could ride a motorcycle.
I wish I was a parrot.
I wish I had a million dollars.
I wish I was a star.

"Five Senses" poems are usually five lines long. These poems are written about a specific topic using each of the five senses, with one line of the poem devoted to each separate sense (Tompkins, 2002). A small group of students wrote the following "Five Senses" poem about spring:

Smells like fresh air.
Tastes like sweet corn.
Looks like red roses.
Feels like a nice walk.
Sounds like kids playing.

CENTERS

Poems students have written interactively work very well in classroom centers. Students can sequence and illustrate the poetry text. Once the text has been laminated, many "word work" activities can also be done. Students can use overhead pens to circle or mark the high-frequency words or other little words found in the text. Interactive poems can also be copied and placed in poetry folders; students love to read and revisit all of the poems they have enjoyed and written during the year.

CONCLUSION

My students take great pride in hearing their own poems roll off their teacher's tongue, and enjoy hearing them even more as they tickle the tongues of their class-mates. Interactive writing supplies a nonthreatening, structured atmosphere in which children can be creative and successful. Each interactive lesson provides English language development that is suitable for children of all English-speaking abilities. Interactive writing puts the power of the pen in the hands of the students, and leads them on their way toward becoming active writers and poets.

REFERENCES

Koch, K. (1980). *Wishes, lies, and dreams.* New York: Vintage.
Prelutsky, J. (1990). *Something big has been here.* New York: Scholastic.
Silverstein, S. (1974). *Where the sidewalk ends.* New York: HarperCollins.
Tompkins, G. (2002). *Language arts: Content and teaching strategies* (5th ed.). Upper Saddle River, NJ: Merrill/Prentice-Hall.

SCIENCE AND INTERACTIVE WRITING

Andra Christenson

Kids love science. Nothing captures children's interest and the imagination more than the antics of a bumblebee or the explosive results of mixing baking soda and vinegar! The wise teacher who channels this excitement will find many opportunities to motivate children to write. Once they are motivated, interactive writing provides the students the necessary support as they begin to express their observations and ideas about science experiences.

There are many ways that science and interactive writing can be used in the classroom. Reporting science experiments, itemizing collections, interviewing visitors, and describing classroom pets all provide chances for children to write. In this chapter, I focus on a variety of ways that I incorporate interactive writing into science.

When I introduce a new science topic in my classroom, I immerse the children in stories, songs, nonfiction books, charts, and photographs. We often create a chart where we list what we know about the subject, things we want to learn, and things we learn as we study the topic; this graphic organizer is called a KWL chart (Ogle, 1986). I keep the chart posted in the classroom as long as we are focusing on the science unit. I invite children to come up to the easel to help with the writing, and I give the rest of the children small white boards so they can write along with the child who is writing at the easel. We sound out new words and build sentences together. After each sentence is written, we read it aloud. Figure 27 shows a KWL chart about bats generated by a first-grade class.

My students also create word lists for new science topics. As groups visit my reading table, I ask each child to think of a science word to write. I pass out 3 × 5-inch cards and marking pens. I then write with them as we sound out the word. We say the word together and make sure that everyone knows the definition. The child then illustrates the word and adds it to a pocket chart. Word lists can be glued to paper and mounted around the room or hung on rings to make room for a new set of vocabulary in the pocket chart. Children have a great sense of ownership during this process.

FIGURE 27 Student KWL chart about bats.

Bats		
know	**Want To Know**	**Learn**
Some Bats ean fruit Bats have Babies	Where Do Bats Live?	Some Bats Have Fur they are hairy.

OUTDOOR EXPLORATIONS

We are fortunate to have a garden at our school site with space available for a formal garden and temporary containers for growing flowers or vegetables. Children write about common garden tasks, such as planting seeds, harvesting vegetables, weeding, and watering. I prefer working with small groups of children when outside; I rely on parents, my classroom aide, cross-age tutors, and student teachers to provide the extra help.

One successful technique is to divide the students into several small groups that rotate to each station; several of the stations often involve interactive writing. Each station has an adult or a cross-age tutor who leads an activity. A typical lesson might look like this:

Station 1 <u>Interactive writing.</u> Students create labels for different garden plants (see Figure 28). Permanent markers, tape, heavy paper, and sticks are provided.

Station 2 <u>Journal writing.</u> Students draw and write about before and after views of the garden plot. The teacher writes with each child as needed. Science journals, pencils, and crayons are provided.

Station 3 <u>Seed planting.</u> A story about the garden is read, and each student plants a seed in the garden. Seed packets can be designed when students return to class. Steps for planting can be written interactively, illustrated, and sequenced in a pocket chart. Books, seeds, garden tools, and a planting area are provided.

Station 4 <u>Sentence frames.</u> Students write about and illustrate various kinds of plants, leaves, or flowers. For young children, a simple frame can be provided and the name of each plant can be written interactively; for example, "This flower is a _____." Drawing paper, clipboards, and writing materials are provided.

If you don't have a garden area, growing things can be observed in the school grass and shrubbery. Students can write about micro-habitats and creatures they find while on a schoolyard safari. My first graders take several forays per year to discover what is crawling about. We carry homemade clipboards made out of sturdy cardboard and an inexpensive paper clip. The children record what they see by drawing quick sketches and writing down the location and behavior of the animal. One child wrote, "This bug is hiding under the leaf. He doesn't want me to find him." The excitement is high and the talking is nonstop. There will be plenty to write about later when we have settled back in the classroom.

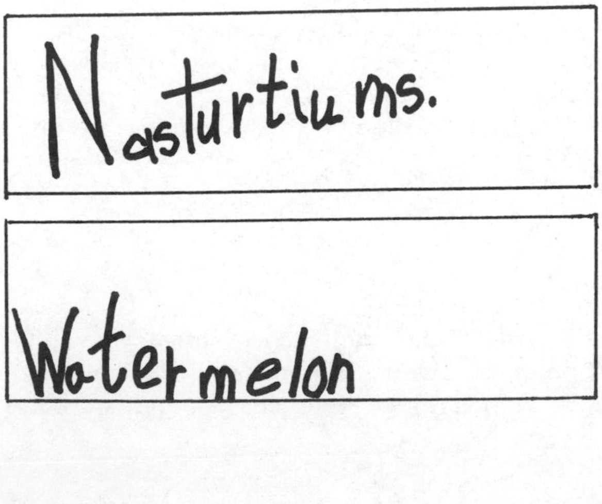

FIGURE 28 Interactively written labels for garden plants.

Nasturtiums.

Watermelon

FIGURE 29 Student notes from field observation.

During the field observations, I divide the class in two groups of 10 students; my aide or a parent volunteer works with one-half of the class and I work with the other. As the children observe the animals, I am moving around and writing interactively with them. I help with a word or an entire sentence, or I simply suggest something to write about. We save the field notes and refer to them later in the classroom. We may write a story about the adventures of a certain insect or make a nonfiction class book. For example, one recent class book written by my first graders was entitled "Insects at Turner Elementary School." As seen in Figure 29, each child drew a picture of a common insect found on our schoolyard and wrote a description.

Drawing or writing in the dirt with a stick or stone is as old as human history; I'm sure we all remember writing our names in the wet sand at the beach or hastily scratching out a hopscotch form on the playground. I was on yard duty one cold day after a rain when I saw several of my students drawing designs on the ground. I walked over to them and picked up a small stick of my own. "Let's see if we can write something in the dirt. You write the words you know and I'll help you with the rest." As we engaged in the writing play, it seemed a perfect time to focus on some informal science. We discussed whether it is better to write in wet or dry soil and why. The children then conducted a search for other great writing spots on the playground.

Another interesting writing medium to use outside is a paintbrush and water. All you need are a container of water and brushes for teacher and child. The child paints the word with the water, and the teacher adds any unknown letters or words. Because water evaporates, you can write anywhere. The questions generated as teacher and child watch their words disappear lead naturally into lessons on the water cycle, evaporation, and weather.

FIELD TRIPS

A recent trip to the zoo provided a perfect opportunity to try interactive writing in a real-life setting. Our parent chaperones arrived a half-hour early for a minilesson on the finer points of interactive writing with 6-year-olds. Parents were each assigned four children, and each group was given the name of a specific animal to observe while at the zoo. The parents also had a science journal for each child, pencils, and a colored marker to use during the visit.

The groups spent the majority of the time just exploring the zoo. After much walking and a lunch break, each group settled down to observe one animal. It is very important to allow children to investigate the new environment before asking them to perform an academic task; they need to satisfy their curiosity and make a mental map of the space before they can focus on reflecting on the space through their writing.

My small group of students studied and wrote about the tiger. We read all the signs around the exhibit. Each child then talked about the information he or she wished to record about the tiger. After sharing with the group, they then wrote independently. I moved from child to child, adding letters and words, if needed. While the more proficient writers were illustrating their pieces, I was able to spend more time with the children who needed extra help. I gave them ideas for possible sentences to write, and we sounded out words and wrote interactively. When the students finished, I collected the journals and the pencils and we continued our zoo visit. The total writing time was 15 minutes.

I took photographs of the children and animals at the zoo. After the film was developed, we wrote captions for the photos interactively and placed them in a pocket chart and later in an album.

CLASSROOM ANIMALS

Despite being in a year-round school, I always have some kind of classroom pet. In the past, I've had fish, rats, guinea pigs, and snails. Temporary visitors such as silkworms and toads pass through, depending on the season or the science theme we are exploring. Students record information in journals, make signs and labels for the cage, create pages for class books, write down questions to research while in the library, and write messages to the animal.

The students work on the writing during our literacy center time. I provide materials and encourage their independent activity. I am able to help each child in between guided reading groups. For example, I recently asked the children to draw a picture of our pet rat and then label the parts of her body. I wrote with them, sounding out words and inserting letters when needed. The finished pieces were displayed around the rat's cage and then bound into a class book.

SCIENCE BIG BOOKS

Students in my classroom use interactive writing to create big books. They create a student-made book in response to a favorite science story; *Jasper's Beanstalk*, by Butterworth and Inkpen (1997), is a class favorite. Children choose a page from the book. They then paint the picture on a 12 × 18 -inch paper. When the painting is dry, I call the students individually to my reading table. I read the text that corresponds to their page of the book. We then write the text interactively without looking at the original text. I use the steps for interactive writing listed in Figure 1 of this book.

As each page is completed, we tape it to the wall at a child's-eye level to create a wall story. The students help with the correct sequencing of the pages. The story is left up to be enjoyed and read until we are ready to replace it with another. Then I compile and staple the pages of the book and it is placed in the big book center. I raffle off books we make at the end of the year.

CONCLUSION

Interactive writing is a natural way to integrate science with the language arts. It is a tool that has helped me strengthen the writing and reading abilities of my students as they learn about science content. The interesting topics found in science provide the motivation to write, and the technique of interactive writing ensures student success and instills in them a belief that they can write.

REFERENCES

Butterworth, N., & Inkpen, M. (1997). *Jasper's beanstalk*. New York: Macmillan/McGraw-Hill.

Ogle, D. M. (1986). K-W-L: A teaching model that develops active reading of expository text. *The Reading Teacher*, 39, 564–570.

Recycled Writing

Theresa Kasner

Making paper is a favorite art activity that I try to fit into my schedule a couple of times a year. But this year, I wanted the children to learn more about the process that we go through to make paper rather than about the final product. I decided to take photos of each step in the process to use with an interactive writing lesson.

Interactive writing is a wonderful activity that can easily be incorporated into any area of the curriculum. Not only do the children feel special about getting to participate in the actual writing, but the knowledge of letters and sounds is reinforced as they think about every sound they hear.

On this particular day, I wanted the students to make orange paper to write their pumpkin list poems on. We had just been on a field trip to the Pumpkin Patch, a local pumpkin store, and each child picked a pumpkin to take back to school. The next day, we looked at our pumpkins and used our five senses as we talked about the different ways we could sort them. We decided to line them up from smallest to largest. Later, in small groups, the children dictated a list poem describing their pumpkin. They also drew a picture of their pumpkin with crayons and covered them with a watercolor wash. There wasn't enough space on the page to write their poems, so I decided to have them make paper on which to write the poem.

We gathered in a circle on the carpet to begin. The students were excited as I began to tell them what we were going to do. I showed them some samples of paper I had made previously. Then I gave each child some orange and white scrap paper and instructed them to tear it up into little pieces. I showed samples of the appropriate size pieces that the blender could break down into pulp.

When they were finished, all the paper was collected in a bag and carried to the paper-making center. The children each took turns placing a handful of scraps into the blender and pushing the button to process the paper, making slurry. As each batch of slurry was made, they dumped it into a large rectangular container. After all children had their turn, it was time to make the paper.

To give each child a chance to make paper, I had centers set up for the children to work at until they were called. One by one, each child came up and lowered the paper-making screen into the container of slurry. After lifting it out, the child used another screen to squeeze out the excess water. Next, the child placed a piece of cotton felt over the paper to blot up the remaining moisture. Then the children took the screen outside and flipped the paper off the screen onto a piece of butcher paper, where it was left to dry.

The next day, they were excited to see their finished products. I also had developed the photos we had taken and placed them in a pocket chart for the children to look at. As a class, we put the photos in the correct order to show the

FIGURE 30 Interactive writing about the paper-making process.

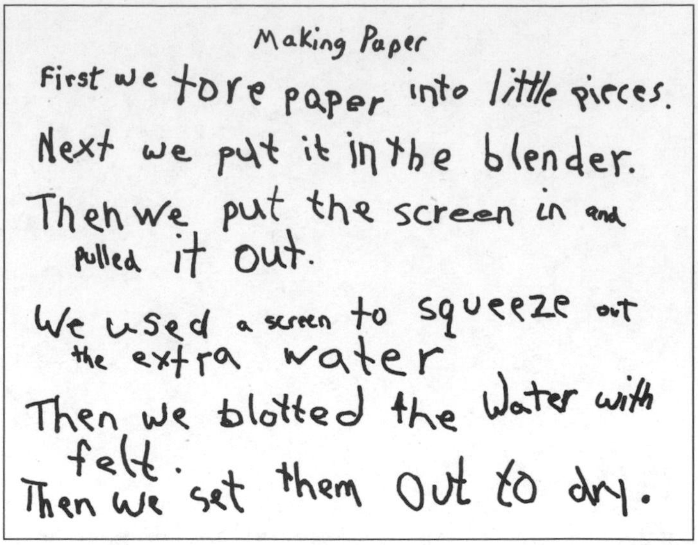

> **Making Paper**
>
> First we tore paper into little pieces.
>
> Next we put it in the blender.
>
> Then we put the screen in and pulled it out.
>
> We used a screen to squeeze out the extra water
>
> Then we blotted the water with felt.
>
> Then we set them out to dry.

sequence that we used to make the paper the previous day. As we talked about each photo, I asked the students to help me write the directions so we would be able to remember how we made the paper.

I explained that we were going to use interactive writing so that everyone could share in the writing process. My children think interactive writing is fun, and they were eager to get started.

When we began the writing activity, the children were sitting on the carpet around the easel. We already had sequenced the photos, so we knew how to write the directions. The first photo showed all the students sitting in a circle tearing paper. I asked them to create a sentence to describe this first step in the paper-making process. They decided to write, *First we ripped up paper scraps into little pieces*. We repeated the sentence and counted out the words on our fingers. Taking turns, each child selected a colored pen and wrote one or two words on the chart.

As each word was written, we repeated the whole sentence to review what we had written and listened for the next word. Before we wrote each word, we stretched the word out slowly, listening for each sound. We often referred to the alphabet chart that is placed right next to the easel for quick reference.

Next, we looked at the pictures in the pocket chart and identified the next step in the process. We repeated these steps until we had written about the entire paper-making process. Our interactive writing is shown in Figure 30.

The next day, I showed the students the sentence strips on which I had written the directions, step by step. As a whole class, we reread the steps. Then we matched the photos to the corresponding step. Next I mixed up all the sentences, and the students sequenced them. One of the choices during center rotation is "reading the room," so I left both the pictures and the sentences in a pocket chart for the students to read during this time.

CONCLUSION

It is very important for the classroom to be filled with things the students have made. Interactive writing is an excellent way to fill the walls with written materials that the students have produced. My students love to reread the things they have written. It gives them a sense of ownership, and it documents our instructional activities.

BEYOND THE PEN: INTERACTIVE WRITING ON THE COMPUTER

Cynthia Schaefer

I've been using interactive writing in my classroom in various forms for the past 9 years, not knowing for most of that time that it even had an official name. During that time, I have taught students in kindergarten through third grade. I believe that interactive writing is the most productive way to empower students as they engage in the process of learning to read and write. It also provides the support students need as they progress toward proficiency, and also provides me with innumerable opportunities to teach skills, concepts, strategies, and procedures in all the areas of language arts.

I began using interactive writing by having my children share their daily news while I recorded it on chart paper. This progressed to a weekly news activity, explained in detail in "Weekly News: Beyond Show and Tell" on p. 35. Throughout the years, as I evaluated and assessed the activities in my classroom, I have refined and changed the ways I use interactive writing. What began with daily news has expanded to finishing frame sentences, completing writing prompts, writing in daily journals, working on class-made stories, recording in math and science journals, and cooperative group assignments. My most recent addition is having students do interactive writing on the computer. Using interactive writing in conjunction with the technology in my classroom has proven to be another beneficial tool for promoting literacy growth and development.

MOVING FROM CHART PAPER TO THE COMPUTER

It bothered me that when the student writing on chart paper stood in front of the writing, the class had trouble seeing clearly what the student and I were putting down on paper. I found myself continually asking the student to step aside—interrupting the student's train of thought—so that I could show the rest of the class the sound, letter, skill, or concept I was explaining and teaching. To alleviate this problem, I moved to the overhead projector for part of our writing time. The students could see the screen, and their view of the writing taking place was unobstructed; however, making corrections was often messy, and the student doing the writing didn't like staring at that bright light.

Finally, we moved to the computer. Voila! I liked the results, and the students loved being able to write using the computer. I don't use computers for all our interactive writing; it really depends on the activity and the purpose for that activity. The chart paper still works best for me with students learning to form their letters and those still working on phonemic awareness and concepts about print. But for older students and those who have mastered basic writing concepts and skills, we were off to the computer.

SETUP AND PROCEDURES

I have a Macintosh computer in my classroom that is connected not only to the regular monitor but also to a television using a cable that takes the video from the computer into the television. The television screen is larger than a monitor and is placed high enough so all students can easily view the text as it is being written on the computer. I use the computer for writing with both the whole class and small groups. With the whole class, the students sit at their seats and often record the text on their own paper as I help one student record on the computer. When I work with small groups, often during literacy centers, the group sits nearer to the television and uses clipboards to do their writing as I work with one student on the computer. Although I am focusing on the student at the computer, I am able to instruct all students by using the pointer or the cursor, or by highlighting specific sections of print on the screen. The entire class benefits from the specific instruction given to this one student.

I have used a variety of word processing programs with interactive writing. I use ClarisWorks and KidWorks 2 most often, but the choice of program depends on the goals and objectives of a particular activity or assignment. In general, any word processing program that you have available will work. The students need basic instruction on using the computer and the word processor, but this is easily done during the interactive writing sessions. As you emphasize which letters in their writing need to be capitalized, you are able to point out and explain the use of the shift key for capitalization. The function of the space bar reinforces the use of spaces between words and helps students to clearly define the separation of words. They learn to make corrections easily by using the backspace key. They are eager to use question marks and exclamation points just to prove to the rest of the class that they know where to find them. Hyphens, commas, and apostrophes are taught as they come up in the negotiated text or student writing. Students quickly learn not only literacy skills and concepts, but they become knowledgeable about basic keyboarding skills as well.

INTERACTIVE WRITING USING THE COMPUTER

I first used interactive writing in conjunction with sharing activities in my classroom that eventually led to the weekly news. Not only did I want everyone to be able to view the writing and benefit from the teaching that was taking place, but I wanted my students to be able to type their own entries for the news. As we moved to the computer to accomplish these goals, we began by typing our weekly news items on the computer. This later expanded to class-made books, collaborative stories, class reports and projects, and using the Internet and a digital camera.

By the time we begin using the computer, the students are already very familiar with the interactive writing process. We have worked our way through modeled writing, where I demonstrate to the students what to share, how to share, and how to write their shared items. We have also gone through the shared writing process, where students become more involved by sharing their thoughts and ideas and negotiating the text with me. Thus, we approach the computer when the students are ready to take the pen in hand and do some of their own writing with my support. But instead of picking up a pen, we sit down in front of the keyboard.

I work with one student at the keyboard while the others watch, listen, and write from their seats. I follow the steps for interactive writing that are found in Figure 1 on page 3. The student tells me what he or she wants to share and I repeat it, making any necessary grammatical corrections or asking clarifying questions. I use these repetitions of text to develop all students' language, especially English language learners. I then repeat the text again, and this time the student and the entire class repeat it after me. We say the text for a third time and count the number of words that were said and will be recorded.

The student now begins typing the text on the computer while the rest of the class writes it on paper. This is an important opportunity for me to demonstrate, teach, and support my students. This is the time I look for teachable moments so I can demonstrate specific skills or concepts in context, as seen in the following example. One student shares, "Andrew's mom is taking him to the baseball game on Saturday." To begin, he types, "Andrews mom," but does not add an apostrophe. I quickly take a moment to talk about apostrophes and how to use them. Then I go back and add it in the text. When I make corrections, I usually use italics or boldface type so that my additions and corrections stand out and this piece of writing can be used later for assessment.

When we finish typing the entire text, the student then reads it to me, pointing to each word on the computer monitor. Next the student uses a pointer on the television screen and reads the text to the entire class. Finally, the student points to the words while the class, looking at the television, reads the text aloud. The students who have written at their seats have had additional practice and reinforcement.

At this time, another student comes to the computer to type his or her news. Once again, we negotiate the text and work through the previous steps. I divide the students in my class into five groups. Each day, the students from one group share and write their news, so by the end of the week, all students have had an opportunity to share and type their news. On Friday, we are ready to publish our weekly news.

I also use the computer for class-made stories and collaborative work. The process is basically the same. After doing prewriting activities, we are ready to begin writing the story. We turn our attention to the computer and the television screen. As we negotiate the text, I choose different students to record each sentence on the computer; the rest of the class helps by repeating the words, correcting spellings, reminding the student to add punctuation, and rereading the text frequently. I either sit nearby and help the student at the computer, or walk around the room finding teachable moments and instructing the whole class. Sometimes when the student at the computer needs help, I will call on another student to go up and help at the computer.

My students also use the computer to access the Internet. The students find pictures on the Internet to coordinate with the themes or specific topics we are studying. For example, as we were studying animals, we downloaded many pictures of elephants, giraffes, zebras, and other animals. The students referred to these pictures as we wrote descriptions of what we saw, wrote facts about the animal, and sometimes made up a short story about that animal; we put the picture of the animal at the top of the television screen and typed the text underneath using interactive writing. These pictures and text can then be used in ClarisWorks, HyperStudio, or other related software to create a slide show or report for presentation to the whole class, other classes, or parents.

Figure 31 shows the first paragraph from a class-made story that combines the use of the Internet and interactive writing. The class worked collaboratively on a story about a pirate ship that ended up on a desert island after encountering a severe storm. While negotiating the text and developing the story, we often draw illustrations to help us visualize what is happening. As I looked at the pictures, I realized most of the students had no idea what a pirate ship looked like. I quickly went to the Internet and had the students search for pirate ships. We found the sketch, downloaded it, and

FIGURE 31 Class story combining the use of the Internet and interactive writing.

Once upon a time there was a pirate ship out sailing the Seven Seas looking for treasure. One day there was a terrible storm. There were big old clouds in the sky and it got very dark. The wind began to blow and the rain came pouring down as huge waves crashed into the side of the boat.

put it at the beginning of our story. This added a new dimension to the story and sparked more creativity and interest from the students.

One other technology tool that I connect with interactive writing is the digital camera. "A Picture Is Worth a Thousand Words" on page 42 explains in detail how to use pictures and interactive writing to stimulate writing. Following those same basic procedures, I move to the computer once again. With the digital camera, students take pictures that are quickly transferred to the computer; putting the camera in their hands gives them a sense of power and ownership. These pictures are then used in ways similar to those downloaded from the Internet. As a picture is displayed on the television screen, the students are extremely excited about seeing themselves up on the television. This creates an environment for meaningful language to occur as they are talking about the pictures, discussing and negotiating the text they will add. I often do this activity with small groups, so the students can create mini–slide shows to present to the rest of the class.

CONCLUSION

The use of technology in the classroom provides many new opportunities to students to develop into proficient readers and writers. As the students are actively engaged in the learning process, they use all six of the language arts: They are learning to write as they put their thoughts into spoken words and then into written words recorded on paper or on the computer; they are learning to listen carefully to themselves, the teacher, and other students as they work cooperatively on many of these activities; they are learning to speak as they share their thoughts and ideas, negotiating text and developing language skills; they are learning to read from purposeful, meaningful text that they and their classmates have created; they are learning to visually represent their thoughts and ideas by using text, photographs, illustrations, and various other tools; and finally, they are learning to meaningfully view the pictures, text, and projects they and others have created.

Interactive writing used with or without the computer has proven to be an indispensable part of my classroom. It allows me to teach directly to the needs of each student while actively engaging students in the learning process. It provides the scaffolding necessary for all students as they take risks and progress through the various stages of reading and writing. The student-generated text is not only meaningful to the students, it enables them to be involved in daily purposeful reading, writing, speaking, and listening across the curriculum.

INTERACTIVE WRITING AND THE WRITING PROCESS

Michelle Crippen

Teaching the writing process is very difficult. It is not something you can simply tell students how to do; instead, teachers must model the process writers use and then provide opportunities for guided practice. I have found that interactive writing is a very useful way to teach the writing process because it takes the learning one step further by giving students an active part in the modeling phase and, therefore, helps them develop a deeper understanding of the process.

PREWRITING

Prewriting is the first stage of the writing process, and it involves choosing a topic, generating ideas, and considering the form, purpose, and audience (Tompkins, 2002). There are many forms of prewriting: clustering, mapping, illustrating, discussing, quick writing, role-playing, and reading. Modeling is good; however, through interactive writing, I model and involve students in the process. A group setting is a wonderful opportunity for students to dialogue about their story ideas; they practice storytelling as they exchange ideas and elaborate on each other's creations. We also interactively create illustrations as a prewriting strategy; the pictures are beneficial for students to visualize a character or setting prior to writing. All students participate in creating a drawing that represents an element of the class story. Clustering is also easily introduced through an interactive format. When students take an active role in the prewriting, their understanding is deepened and they are better prepared to practice the strategy independently.

While preparing to write a class story about friendship, my students interactively created a cluster of ideas about friends. Each child took shared ideas about friendship, using the pen to write words onto a chart. Many ideas were generated during the discussion as the students decided on a plan for their writing. The students then interactively completed a story map involving all the characteristics they had previously learned about story writing. Several days were dedicated to the prewriting process to allow for all students to be involved. Figures 32 and 33 show the prewriting.

Whichever form of prewriting is used for the class story, my students also use this form to prewrite independently for their individual stories. After making a cluster with the group, my students then apply what they have practiced in their own writing. Students each created a cluster and a story map around the common topic, friendship. A sample cluster is shown in Figure 34 and a sample story map in Figure 35.

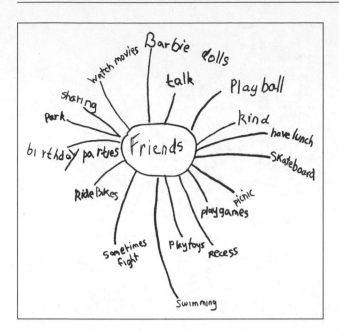

FIGURE 32 Cluster of ideas about friends.

FIGURE 33 Story map about Mrs. Crippen.

Beginning	Middle	End
Character: Mrs. Crippen	problem gets worse or	Solution:
glasses	more problems occur:	She tried to climb the fen Got stuck Lupe helps
Blond hair		
Blurry eyes	Can't find keys	
teaches helps	has to sleep there	
Reads "Where's my angels?"	thrashed up the room	
feels sad when books are	She could not eat or read books falls apart	
Setting: damaged	Room	happy ending.
Miramonte	No One to take	"Thank you Lupe"
Valentine's Day	care of Cameron	went home got cameron
	She tried the phone mad at self	Camerton had keys
Problem:	Can see keys out the window	
Mrs. Crippen gets locked in the school	brakes window	

DRAFTING

In the drafting stage of the writing process, students "pour out their ideas with little concern about spelling, punctuation, and other mechanical aspects of writing" (Tompkins, 2002, p. 117). My class spends a few days developing a draft of their class story. We chunk the story into parts such as beginning, middle, and end or character, setting, problem, and solution. We work on each part for a day. I watch the children to determine timing. I do not continue until students lose interest; rather, I stop when the children are still eager to return to their story at a later time. I model how ideas are generated as we sketch out our draft onto the paper interactively. I do not overemphasize grammar and punctuation. During an interactive story-writing activity, I assist students with the spelling of words by using a different colored marker and correction tape. However, I leave the capitalization and punctuation errors for the editing phase of the process.

FIGURE 34 Student-generated cluster about a friend.

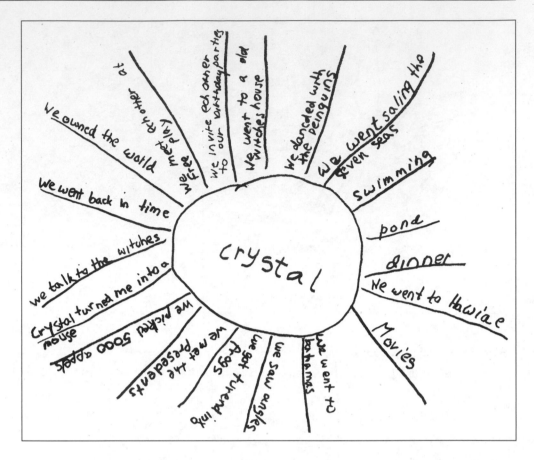

FIGURE 35 Student story map about a friend.

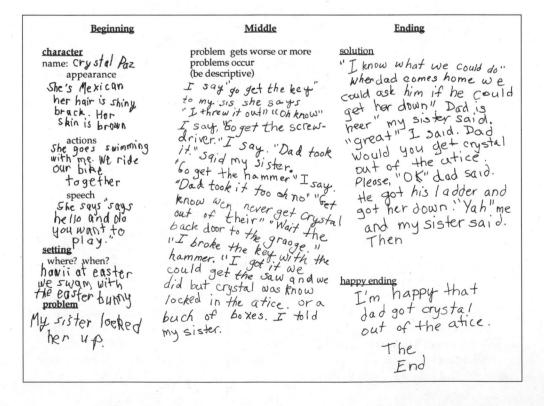

The class draft of our friendship story took several days. We divided the story into beginning, middle, and end; each portion of the story took at least 2 days to complete. Everyone contributed to the ideas and sentences as we referred to our story map. The students added creativity, description, and flavor to their story each step of the way.

After working on the class draft, my students returned to their personal prewriting maps to begin developing their drafts. They had seen and participated in drafting with the group and therefore had ownership of the process; they were better prepared to begin a draft of their own. As the class draft began to take form, so did the individual drafts the students were creating independently. Figure 36 illustrates a paragraph from one child's draft in which she wrote about her friend, Alyssa.

REVISING

Revision requires writers to "see again" what they have written and to refine their ideas. During the revision phase, writers focus on adding, deleting, substituting, and moving ideas within the piece. Common activities include rereading, sharing, and conferencing (Tompkins, 2002). In my class, revising takes place as the group makes decisions about the writing piece. I emphasize with the students that we are looking at the message of the story, not the mechanics. They work on adding, deleting, moving, or substituting words and ideas in their draft. The class also decides who will view their draft and offer suggestions for revision; this may be students from another class, a teacher, or the principal, depending on class preference. At times the draft is also cut apart to enable students to move a paragraph or section of the story to a different location.

After putting our friendship drafts away for 2 weeks, we were able to "see again" with fresh eyes. The class worked at adding new ideas, deleting some that did not belong, substituting new ideas for old ones, and moving the text around. We invited other students into our classroom to give feedback on the story as we revised further. Figure 37 is a revised sample from our class story.

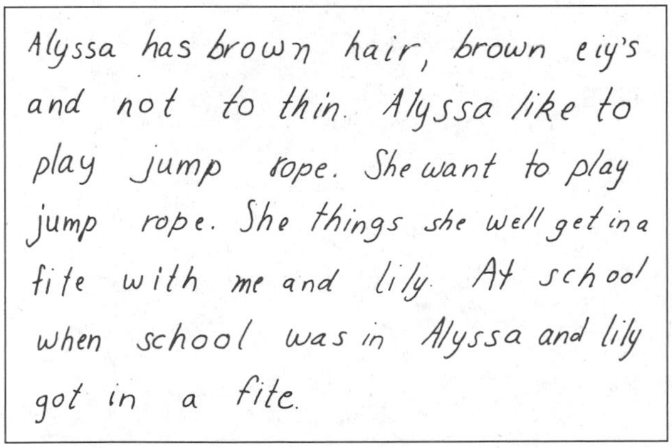
Alyssa has brown hair, brown eiy's and not to thin. Alyssa like to play jump rope. She want to play jump rope. She things she well get in a fite with me and lily. At school when school was in Alyssa and lily got in a fite.

FIGURE 36 Student's first draft about a friend.

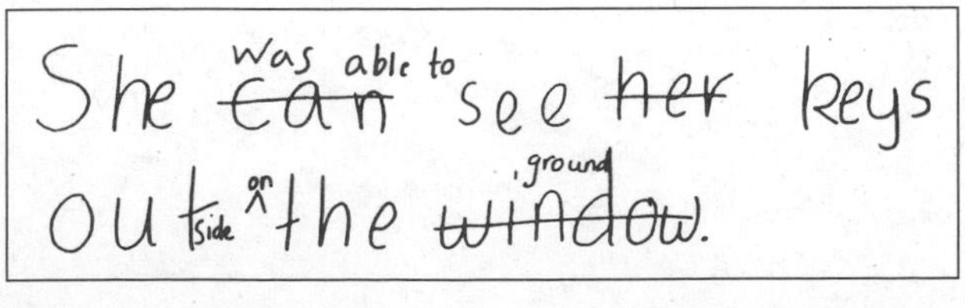
She ~~can~~ was able to see ~~her~~ keys out side on the ~~window~~ ground.

FIGURE 37 Revised version of class story.

After completing this process on the class story, my students had a solid understanding of what was necessary in revising their own writing. They began to revise by cutting, erasing, taping, and inserting changes into their stories with little concern for punctuation or grammar. Following a period of individual revision, the students selected someone to peer revise their story as well. As experienced group and individual revisers, my students were better equipped to offer revision assistance to others. Figure 38 is a sample of a child's revised writing.

EDITING

Editing is cleaning up the piece by correcting all misspellings and other mechanical errors. Our purpose was to prepare our story for publishing and ensure it was readable. I began each editing session with a minilesson on an editing skill. As we approached the writing, we first searched for any corrections related to the new skill. Next, we edited the piece for all previously taught editing concepts. This was a great opportunity for review.

Before viewing the class story, I taught a minilesson on possessive 's. When we returned to the class story, we looked for and corrected errors involving possessive 's. We then searched for other errors in concepts we had previously learned, including capitalization rules, punctuation marks, and grammar skills.

Students returned to their individual writing to look for errors; they knew they were to edit using the new editing skill as well as all previously taught skills. Students also each selected a peer editing partner or group to check for any further errors. Peer editing is great editing practice because students are

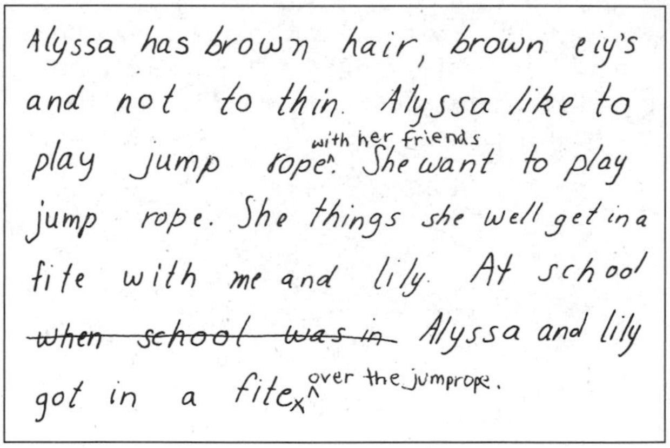
Alyssa has brown hair, brown eiy's
and not to thin. Alyssa like to
play jump rope. with her friends She want to play
jump rope. She things she well get in a
fite with me and lily. At school
~~when school was in~~ Alyssa and lily
got in a fite over the jumprope.

FIGURE 38 Student's revised writing about a friend.

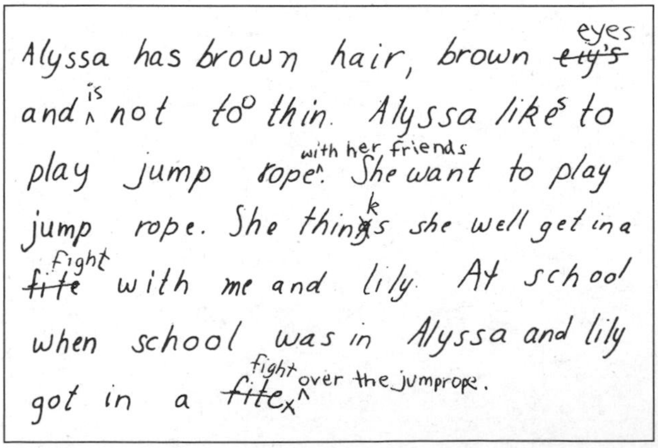
Alyssa has brown hair, brown ~~eiy's~~ eyes
and is not too thin. Alyssa likes to
play jump rope. with her friends She want to play
jump rope. She thinks she well get in a
~~fite~~ fight with me and lily. At school
when school was in Alyssa and lily
got in a ~~fite~~ fight over the jumprope.

FIGURE 39 Student's edited writing about a friend.

not as familiar with their partner's writing. I also held editing conferences in which I used teachable moments to reinforce editing concepts. Figure 39 is a student editing sample.

PUBLISHING

Students bring their compositions to life during the publishing stage. They may publish on charts or in books, or share them orally with an appropriate audience. This stage is important because "through sharing their writing with real audiences . . . students come to think of themselves as authors" (Tompkins, 2002, p. 123). Publishing can be done in many ways, such as newspapers, big books, pop-up books, charts, and flip books. For the publication to be done interactively, all students must be involved in the creation.

All students took part in rewriting the friendship story in book form. We used a computer, enabling all students to take part in typing the class story and developing keyboarding skills. As students took turns typing, the class viewed the text on a large screen or TV monitor. The group identified and corrected errors. Once the text was written or typed, my students broke into small groups to illustrate parts or pages of the class story. Figure 40 is a page from the published class book.

Students then published their individual stories in a similar fashion. A variety of ways presented throughout the year allowed students to choose their own form for their personal published book. Figure 41 is a page from a child's published book.

CONCLUSION

Interactive writing is invaluable when introducing the stages of the writing process, providing guided practice, and teaching new concepts in writing. Through direct modeling, my students practice the steps of the writing process as they create class stories. Simultaneously, they develop their own stories as each new step is introduced and practiced. This allows for an immediate opportunity for my students to individually put into practice what they have learned with the group.

Our teacher's name is Mrs. Crippen. She has a son named Cameron. She has glasses, blond hair and blurry eyes. She likes to teach and help others. She loves reading and always calls her students her little angels. She feels sad when books are damaged. One day at Miramonte Elementary School, Mrs. Crippen got locked in her classroom. She couldn't find her keys anywhere.

FIGURE 40   Page from published class book.

FIGURE 41 Page from a student's published book.

My friend's name is Crystal. She is Mexican.
Her hair is golden shiny black and her skin is brown.
She goes swimming with me all the time. We ride
our bikes together. She says "Hello" to me every
morning. She always asks, "Do you want to play?"
She feels happy because she has a friend like me.

REFERENCE

Tompkins, G. (2002). *Language arts: Content and teaching strategies* (5th ed.). Upper Saddle River, NJ: Merrill/Prentice Hall.

USING INTERACTIVE WRITING TO TEACH REVISION: TWO APPROACHES

Theresa Kasner

Students often think their writing is finished once they write the last sentence on their papers. This seems to be true every year in my second-grade classroom as the students quickly say, "I'm done!" It is at this stage that my work in teaching writing truly begins.

One of my major roles as a teacher of writing is to get students to revisit their piece to make it better, to make it come alive through the use of the revising stage of the writing process. Revising, often confused with editing, is one of the most important stages in the writing process: This is the stage where students learn to bring a piece of writing to life.

The writing process is composed of five stages: prewriting, writing, revising, editing, and publishing. During the revising stage, ideas are refined to provide the reader with a clear and complete picture. There are four types of revision: substitutions, additions, deletions, and rearrangement of text.

One way I have found to help my students see how the revision process works is to combine revision with an interactive writing activity. I have developed two approaches that have been extremely successful: One method involves the use of a pocket chart and text that can be manipulated, and the other uses a computer to show how text can be added and manipulated easily on the screen. These methods provide a whole-class lesson showing in a nonthreatening way how simple text can be changed, making it come alive with vivid words and descriptive images.

LESSON 1 : REVISION IN THE POCKET CHART

During this process of revision, text written on sentence strips is placed in a pocket chart. I begin with a basic story or report of information. As a group, we add new text using interactive writing, with the children taking turns sharing the pen to write words on cut-up sentence strips. Deletions or substitutions easily take place by removing words and replacing them with the new text. I have used this method with both whole classes and small groups.

One specific activity took place during our study of the desert. We were studying the plant life found in the deserts of the United States; the class was very interested in one plant found in the Sonoran Desert called the saguaro, often referred to as "the desert giant." We read many books and watched a video about this unique plant.

Figure 42 Finished class report in the pocket chart.

The	saguaro	cactus	grows	in	the	**great**	**Sonoran**	desert.
The	**Sonoran**	**desert**	**is**	**in**	**the**	**southwestern**	**part**	**of**
the	**US.**	~~It~~	**When**	**the**	**cactus**	**is**	**75**	**years**	**old**	**it**	**begins**
to	grow	arms.	~~Some~~	~~animals~~	~~live~~	**The**	**Gila**	**Woodpecker**	**and**
the	**Elf**	**Owl**	**make**	**their**	**homes**	**in**	the	saguaro.	**First**	**the**
woodpecker	**makes**	**a**	**hole**	**and**	**uses**	**it**	**for**	**a**	**nest.**	**Later**
the	**elf**	**owl**	**moves**	**in**	**and**	**lives**	**there.**	~~They~~	**Saguaro's**
can	go	without	water	for	a	long	time	**because**	**they**	**store**	**it**
up	**inside.**	**They**	**live**	**for**	**up**	**to**	**200**	**years.**	~~a~~	~~long~~	~~time~~
They	**are**	**the**	**giants**	**of**	**the**	**desert.**

We looked at a young saguaro cactus and other types of cacti to observe their characteristics. I also led a directed drawing lesson on the saguaro.

After our study, I wrote some of the information about the saguaro on sentence strips and placed them in the pocket chart. The next day, I gathered the students together to read what I had written. They said that I left out many great facts. Together as a class, we began to go over what I had written to add more details. We read one sentence at a time and discussed what words we could add to make the sentence more interesting. The first sentence was *The saguaro cactus grows in the desert.* One student said that we should say the "Sonoran Desert." Another added that we should say the "Great Sonoran Desert" because that was what it was called in the video. Still another student wanted to add the words "southwestern part of the United States" so we would know the geographical location.

The process continued as the students took turns writing words on sentence strip pieces using the interactive writing techniques of stretching out the word to hear each sound. During this step, we reviewed phonics rules and the concept that not all words can be sounded out. If we had a nonphonetic word, the student looked it up in a dictionary.

We continued until the students felt that we had added enough information to make the report more complete. Figure 42 shows an example of our finished report.

The students decided that they would each like a copy of the final report to glue onto the back of their paintings of the saguaro. I typed up the final draft, leaving out what needed to be deleted and incorporating the changes the students suggested.

The students wanted to share their research with another class, so I divided them into three groups to practice reading the finished report. When they were ready, they presented their reports to the three first-grade classrooms. The students were very excited and did a wonderful job. That day they were anxious to take their reports home to share with their families.

LESSON 2: REVISION USING THE COMPUTER

This activity was done as a whole group by connecting a computer to a television via an audio/visual (AV) box. The AV box made the text large enough so all students could see the computer screen. An AV box can be purchased at any computer store for around $25 and easily set up in the classroom. This is a relatively simple task and well worth the expense and effort. The computer then becomes a tool that can be used for whole-class instruction. Otherwise, I recommend teaching the lesson to small groups.

I began our revision lesson by sharing a very simple piece of text that I had written on the computer. First we read it as a class:

> One day I went for a walk. I saw a fairy. It flew down by me. I screamed. I went home and told my mom. She said I must have been dreaming.

We agreed that my story needed to have more details. The students told me I hadn't written enough details to give them a visual image of what had actually happened, so I asked them to help me to make my story more exciting. They began to ask me questions about my writing, starting with the first sentence: *One day I went for a walk.* They asked what type of day it was. I asked them to think about what the weather might have been like. They decided to make it a warm, bright, sunny day.

Before the first student came up to type, we had a brief lesson on basic computer skills, such as what a cursor is and how to move it within the text on the screen. I also taught them how to fix mistakes by pressing the arrow keys. I demonstrated how to bold the new text so that we could keep track of what the students added. One student sat at the computer and moved the cursor to the correct position to begin to add the new words. Before the students added new words, we stretched out the sounds of each word, spelling it aloud.

For the first word, *sunny,* we talked about the different ways to spell the long *e* sound at the end of a word. We also talked about why a comma is needed when making a list of words. One student said that without the comma, we would have to write *a warm and bright and sunny day.*

Next we discussed the places where I might have taken a walk. The students suggested "in the mountains," "by the creek," and "to the park," and then agreed to add the phrase *to the park.* Another student came to the keyboard and typed in the new words. We discussed the correct homophone to use for *to,* and that *the* was one of their automatic words. Next, we stretched out the sounds for the word *park.* Referring to our *r*-controlled word list from an earlier lesson, we looked to see which letter combination spelled the /ar/ sound.

This process continued as we added more descriptive words to the story. Soon the first two sentences were complete, and we reread them as a class: *One warm, bright, sunny day I took a walk to the park. I saw a big, ugly, hairy fairy in a tall pine tree.*

When we came to the next sentence, one boy responded that the sentence should be "the fairy jumped down from the tree," so I asked him to explain his reasoning. He said that the fairy was too big and his wings were too little for him to fly. We all laughed as he demonstrated how little the wings were. By this time, the students decided it should be a boy fairy; I don't know if there is such a thing, but it was their decision.

When the next student came up to type, I pointed out how to highlight and delete words within text. The word *flew* was deleted by highlighting the word and using the strike-through tool under the style column, and *jumped* was typed in its place. One student added that the fairy jumped down by my foot.

Next, I asked the students to suggest some reasons why I would scream. They responded with many different ideas, but we settled on adding *and kissed me on the hand with his big, green, slimy lips.* The students reminded the new typist to add the commas between the words in the list so he wouldn't have to add so many *and*'s. As each word was added, the class continued to stretch out the sounds and I discussed spelling rules and concepts that applied to words they wrote.

I asked them how loud they would scream if a big, ugly, hairy fairy kissed them on the hand with his big, green, slimy lips. This brought up some wonderful comments, such as "I screamed so loud that the dead could hear me," and "even the deaf could hear me scream." We settled on I *screamed so loud they could hear me all the way to Mexico.*

FIGURE 43 Completed story written interactively on the computer.

One **warm, bright, sunny** day I went for a walk **to the park.** I saw a **big, ugly, hairy** fairy **in a gigantic pine tree.** It ~~flew~~ **jumped from the tree, because its body was too big for its miniature wings.** ~~down by me.~~ **It kissed me on the hand with his green, ugly, slimy lips.** I screamed **so loud they could hear me all the way to Mexico.** I ~~went~~ **ran** home **as fast as a freight train.** I ~~and~~ told my mom **and** she said, **"There are no such things as fairies! You** ~~I~~ **must have been day** dreaming. I said, **"Yes there are. Look at my hand. I still have the kiss mark from his big, green, slimy lips." But when I looked at my hand it was gone. Maybe it was all a dream.**

The lesson continued as we talked about computer skills, phonics and language rules, interactive writing, and the revision process while the students actively brought the piece to life with wonderful, vivid, visual descriptions. Their completed, revised story can be seen in Figure 43. When our revised story was completed, we removed all the revision marks and decided how to divide up the text into separate pages, keeping the meaning of the story clear. Together we decided what the fairy and the girl looked like so the illustrations would match. Working with partners, the students completed their pages for the final product, a collaborative class book for all to share.

CONCLUSION

Interactive writing is a wonderful process that enables students to actively participate in the revision process. It is a nonthreatening approach to a process that can otherwise bring tears of frustration to the eyes of many young children. Students are often so set on the idea that their writing is fine just the way it is that they are hesitant to revisit and improve a written piece. I observed a big change in my students' abilities to revise after they actively participated in this process the first time. They began to question each other so that they could create a more interesting and complete story, and our process was playful and interactive.

USING INTERACTIVE WRITING AS AN ASSESSMENT TOOL

Michelle Crippen

Interactive writing plays many roles in my classroom. One of these roles is assessment: I use interactive writing to identify and target my students' instructional needs. Each interactive writing experience gives me valuable information about my students' understanding of language, as well as skills that need to be taught or reviewed. I also use interactive writing as an opportunity to discover new and challenging skills students are ready to experiment with in their writing.

I began using interactive writing for assessment when I was asking myself, "Am I really teaching skills?" I used sticky notes to illustrate evidence of the number of concepts and the range of abilities covered in one interactive writing lesson. Also, I wanted to demonstrate to myself how interactive writing reaches across ability levels; the interactive writing lesson has allowed me to assist students who are struggling with beginning writing skills as well as stretch and expand the skills of advanced writers.

Not only did I identify a wide variety of concepts, but I also had valuable documentation of my students' needs. The results amazed me! From a 30-minute interactive writing lesson, I documented approximately 20 concepts created from teachable moments; the skills I covered included the formation of letters, letter reversals, capitalization rules, spelling, periods, quotation marks, and 's. I have continued to use the sticky notes for whole-class, small-group, and individual assessments during interactive writing lessons.

In this chapter, I outline how interactive writing can be used for assessment during whole-class lessons, small-group experiences, and individual writing. I also describe a sample lesson in which I gathered individual assessment information from a small-group interactive writing lesson on how to write a friendly letter.

WHOLE-CLASS ASSESSMENT

During a whole-class interactive writing lesson, I keep a black marker, correction tape, and a small pad of sticky notes on hand. While students are developing a piece of writing, I fill in words or letters, when needed, using the black marker; this allows me to see how much teacher assistance was needed during the writing. My students use correction tape and colored markers to self-correct errors. I also use the tape to help with any necessary corrections. Throughout the experience, I jot down notes on sticky notes about each skill with which the children needed assistance. For example, when a student writes *i* instead of I, I help the child correct the error and write "cap. the word I" on a sticky note. My notes are usually condensed or abbreviated and take only a

FIGURE 44   Whole-class assessment of writing using sticky notes.

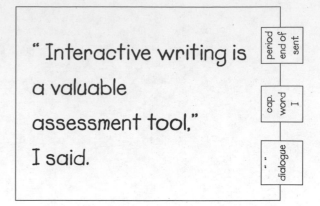

brief moment to write; the note taking does not interrupt the flow of the lesson. I attach the sticky notes along the side of the interactive writing piece, as shown in Figure 44.

Following the lesson, I review the sticky notes to determine writing skills on which I need to focus, and I use this information to develop subsequent writing lessons. I keep a listing of skills on a database or chart that compares occurrences of errors from one interactive writing lesson to another.

SMALL-GROUP ASSESSMENT

I also use small, homogeneous groups for interactive writing because it allows me to focus on the needs of particular students; the range of needs, skills, and abilities of an entire class can be immense. By dividing students into homogeneous groups for interactive writing lessons, I can focus on specific skills that are appropriate for that group of students. The sticky notes from a small-group lesson highlight the specific needs of students with similar writing skills. I then prepare and teach minilessons for this particular group of children.

INDIVIDUAL ASSESSMENT

Individual interactive writing experiences also provide me with valuable information about students' writing abilities. By using a black pen and a colored marker while writing, I can clearly identify areas where the student is dependent on my assistance. I take notes in the form of anecdotal records or write on sticky tablets for the student's file.

Individual interactive writing, however, takes a great deal of time. Because I do not always have time to write one-on-one with my students, I found a way to gather individual assessments through whole-class and small-group interactive writing lessons: During these lessons, I continue with the same procedure outlined earlier, but I also add the initials or name of the child who was involved in the interactive writing on the sticky notes. For example:

> quotation marks in dialogue
> Mark T.

At the end of a lesson, I can pull sticky notes from the chart and sort them into groups by skill. I use a grouping form to divide students by skill focus. I can then plan and prepare lessons for individual groups of students with similar needs.

FIGURE 45 List of skills covered in minilessons.

```
                    Sheet for Organizing Skill Instruction

Lesson: Friendly Letter                                    Date: _____

skill: ___finish a line___   skill: __space between words__   skill: __period at end of sentence__
                                      &/or sentences

        Ming                            Timmy                          Nicholas
        Timmy                           Ming


skill: ___indenting a new___  skill: ___comma in greeting___  skill: __capitalization rules__
       paragraph                       &/or closing                   review

        Katrina                         Jose                           Timmy
        Lee                             Crystal                        Joanna
        Jose                            Sam
                                        Fred


skill: _____       skill: _____         skill: _____
```

A SAMPLE LESSON: HOW TO WRITE A FRIENDLY LETTER

Following a lesson on writing a friendly letter, my students composed a thank-you note to a teacher who allowed us to use her classroom for Writers' Camp. The interactive writing served as the guided practice for the lesson.

The students sat on the floor in front of our chart paper. Together we created the text while reviewing the components of a letter. The class created and recorded the text one sentence at a time. Students worked on Magnadoodles and dry-erase boards on the carpet while one student at a time contributed to the letter. Students created teachable moments as they wrote, asked questions, and made errors.

During the lesson, we reviewed a variety of skills. As each skill was discussed, I made a notation of the skill and a child's name on a sticky note and attached it to the chart. As I noted other students making the same error on their small boards, I added their names to the sticky note. For example:

```
comma in a closing
Timmy, Shelly, Lee
```

Following the lesson, I sorted the sticky notes by skill. Next I planned and prepared minilessons that targeted the needs as seen through the writing lesson. Figure 45 is a completed grouping form listing the skills and lessons that were covered.

CONCLUSION

Interactive writing provides me with many opportunities for direct modeling and explicit teaching. The skills covered in a lesson are numerous, broad, and targeted at my students' needs. By using sticky notes during the interactive writing experience, I walk away with valuable information about what my students know and what they need to learn.

DARLENA: PORTRAIT OF AN EMERGENT WRITER

Stephanie Collom

It is our responsibility to help students stretch their abilities as far as possible to reach their full potential, supporting their development in every way we can. According to Vygotsky (1978, p. 85), "what children can do with the assistance of others might be in some sense even more indicative of their mental development than what they can do alone." By scaffolding students' thinking processes through the use of interactive writing, teachers work with students in their "zone of proximal development." According to Vygotsky, teachers support children in making the speaking/reading/writing connection in a more meaningful way, and help them to apply their new knowledge in their independent work. This chapter documents the writing development of one child through her kindergarten year in school and demonstrates the power of interactive writing.

Emergent writers move along a developmental continuum. The stages, as defined by Routman (1991) and Gentry and Gillet (1993), are:

1. *Picture writing.* The student uses a picture to represent writing; no letters or scribbles are used.

Translation: my house

2. *Scribble writing.* The student differentiates between the picture and the writing, but no letters are used.

Translation: I see the tree.

3. *Precommunicative spelling.* The student differentiates between the picture and writing, and letters are randomly used to represent writing. The letters do not correlate to the sounds in the words.

H l o t m r

Translation: This is my bike.

4. *Semiphonetic spelling*. The student uses initial consonants to represent words.

I L m C

Translation: I love my cat.

5. *Phonetic spelling*. The student successfully conveys a message and may use beginning and ending consonants, usually writing more than one letter to represent a word. The student may also use temporary spelling for some words and conventional spelling for high-frequency words.

I hv a kat

Translation: I have a cat.

6. *Transitional spelling*. The student uses basic conventions of spelling but may reverse some letters or substitute letters with the same sounds.

To dae is my Brith Dae.

Translation: Today is my birthday.

When students are given support and instruction through the interactive writing process, they are better able to progress through these developmental writing stages. My kindergarten students proceed through these stages in their independent writing, but since incorporating interactive writing into my daily classroom activities, I have seen them progress through the continuum much more rapidly. Through interactive writing, they see the reading/writing connection sooner. They are able to apply what they learn about sound/symbol relationships during their interactive writing experiences into their independent writing activities.

One student in my class, Darlena, entered kindergarten with very little literacy experience. She did not attend preschool, and her parents are Cambodian immigrants who are in the preproduction stage of English. She has three older siblings who speak, read, and write in English with varying degrees of proficiency. Darlena started the school year in August at the preproduction stage of English oral language development, and she was able to communicate some of her basic needs and wants. She was at the emergent stage in English literacy development. She was not able to identify any letters or sounds, and she used random letters to write her name, except for a "D" at the beginning. Darlena also used random letters in her independent writing, but differentiated between the picture and the writing. When asked to read her writing, she usually did not respond, or she pointed to the picture.

I started the year by using activities that focused on the letters in the students' names. Darlena very quickly learned to write her name and to recognize the letters in her name. In September, when most of the students were becoming familiar with the letters in their names, I introduced interactive writing during our daily diary time. With the whole class gathered on the carpet, we would discuss what we had learned that day. We would decide on a sentence to write, and I would invite students to come up and write in the letters they knew in each word. For example, if we were going to write the word *made*, we would slowly say the word together, and I would prompt the students by saying, "Listen to the beginning sound in *made*. That sounds like the beginning sound in *Mario*." Then Mario would come up and fill in the *m* in our word. Very soon, every time Darlena would hear a /d/ in a word, her hand would shoot up and she would fill in the letter *d*. Through our daily diary activity, she also learned the letters and sounds in the other children's names. During our subsequent interactive writing activities, Darlena very quickly started learning the alphabetic principle and connecting sounds with symbols. She could fill in more and more letters in the words.

I use whole-group, small-group, and individual interactive writing activities daily. After introducing and practicing the interactive writing process with the whole group, I then start working with small groups and individuals. This allows me to monitor their writing progress very closely and plan my whole- and small-group activities to meet class and individual needs. I always have a picture alphabet chart and a class name list available for the students to refer to while they are writing to help with letter formation and identification. In late September, when I saw that most of the students recognized some letters and knew the sounds that were associated with them, I began the small-group and individual interactive writing activities. Because Darlena had already learned some of the letters and sounds for the letters through our daily diary activities, she did not have any difficulty with the small-group activities. If she was not sure of a sound or letter, she would try to think of a student in the class who had that particular sound in his or her name, or she would refer to the picture alphabet chart. Her English vocabulary was also growing rapidly, and she was becoming more willing to share her ideas with others. This is how Darlena wrote *flower*; the letters I wrote are shown in dotted lines, and Darlena's writing is in solid lines.

F L O W e R

Although Darlena could apply her knowledge of letter/sound relationships during our interactive writing sessions, she was not yet putting this knowledge to use in her independent writing. Darlena used random letters to write "the cloud," as this sample shows:

B B I O H t

When I assessed Darlena's letter knowledge in October, I saw that she was able to recognize 35 out of 52 upper- and lowercase letters. Although she did not recognize all the letters in isolation, she was able to remember the letter names during our interactive writing sessions when she could refer to the picture alphabet chart. For example, she wrote the following words during an interactive writing activity:

ViNe   PUMPKiN

oraNge

She identified and wrote all the letters that made a sound that correlated with the letter and sound on the alphabet chart; I wrote only the letters she didn't know. If she could not identify the letter by name, I filled in the letter. She had memorized the spelling of orange from a song we had learned as a class, but she was still using random letters in her independent journal writing. This is how Darlena wrote "the pumpkin patch":

ABDiLE

By December, Darlena could recognize all of the upper- and lowercase letters in isolation. She could also read the following words: I, *a*, *is*, *in*, *am*, and *to*. I "negotiate" the high-frequency words in our daily diary interactive writing work to familiarize the students with the spelling and use of these words. Darlena wrote this sentence during an interactive writing activity:

I See the
DreiDeL.

Darlena was beginning to speak and write in complete sentences, and as her English speaking skills grew, she became more verbal in class and more willing to share her ideas and help others with their independent writing. Her own independent writing began to show some use of letter/sound knowledge. This is how she wrote "a tree and Santa":

AECnT

By April, Darlena could identify all the letter sounds in isolation and could identify additional high-frequency words: *come*, *like*, *see*, *the*, *and*, *it*. Her English speaking skills had grown tremendously, and she was now in the early production stage of English oral language development. She made appropriate oral responses to commands and questions, used basic survival vocabulary, participated in group discussions, and recited simple chants and poems. In our interactive writing activities, she wrote longer, more complex sentences:

They are
PLaYinGON The
GRass.

She was now applying her knowledge of sight words in her independent writing, choosing to write the words that she knew and felt comfortable writing, but not yet willing to take too many risks with unknown words. Her sentence "I like orange" is easy to read:

I like orange.

By June, the end of our school year, Darlena felt very comfortable writing on her own, and she enjoyed sharing her work with others. I was especially pleased that she attempted to write words she did not know how to spell, using her knowledge of sound/symbol relationships to help her figure out how to write the words. Here she wrote "I see the apple," "see kid," and "I see the cars":

I see the APPle

I see the crs see kid

Darlena could write 48 words on her own, according to Clay's writing vocabulary assessment (2002). Her writing demonstrates a more developed vocabulary than her oral language does.

CONCLUSION

According to Vygotsky, "what a child can do with assistance today she will be able to do by herself tomorrow" (1978, p. 87). This is the essence of interactive writing and its effect on a child's writing development. Through teacher support, scaffolding what the children already know, and using prompts such as picture alphabet charts to help them with the unknown, the teacher is forming a base of knowledge the students can then internalize and use in their own independent writing. Darlena's academic growth over the course of her kindergarten year shows what students are capable of doing with the right teacher support and with daily interactive writing.

REFERENCES

Clay, M. M. (2002). *An observation survey of early literacy achievement* (2nd ed.). Portsmouth, NH: Heinemann.

Gentry, J. R., & Gillet, J. W. (1993). *Teaching kids to spell*. Portsmouth, NH: Heinemann.

Routman, R. (1991). *Invitations*. Portsmouth, NH: Heinemann.

Vygotsky, L. S. (1978). *Mind in society: The development of higher psychological processes*. Cambridge, MA: Harvard University Press.

USING INTERACTIVE WRITING WITH OLDER NOVICE WRITERS

Gail Tompkins

Interactive writing is a powerful tool for novice writers, whether they are first graders, fourth graders, or even older. I visited an eighth-grade class in Fresno and had the opportunity to work with a group of seven English language learners. Five of these students were native speakers of Spanish, and the other two were native Hmong speakers. All seven were fluent, conversational English speakers, and they had received literacy instruction in English for 3 years or more; however, they all had difficulty reading and writing.

I worked with these students over a week while their classmates were at the media center researching and writing reports on topics related to the Underground Railroad. These students used interactive writing to compose a group essay on the Underground Railroad, which took an interesting turn quite by accident.

DAY 1: HOW I BEGAN

I began by asking students what they had learned about the Underground Railroad, their social studies unit for the past 5 weeks; I wanted to activate and clarify their background knowledge before beginning to do the interactive writing activity. I wrote key words from what they told me on one section of the chalkboard, which I labeled the "Word Wall." At first they were hesitant, but Armando offered, "It was for the slaves so they could get to freedom," and I wrote *slaves* and *freedom*. Then Ernesto added, "Harriet Tubman, she was the conductor on the Underground Railroad," and I wrote *Harriet Tubman* and *conductor* on the word wall. Mai added, "The slaves looked at the Big Dipper as they walked on the Underground Railroad and they only walked at night so that they could see the stars." I wrote *Big Dipper* and *walked at night* on the word wall. Then I asked if the Underground Railroad was a real railroad, and Graciela giggled and explained, "No, that's just what they called it but it wasn't no railroad." I wrote "not a real railroad" on the word wall. I waited for another comment. I waited and waited. Finally, I asked, "Where were they going?" and Juan immediately answered with confidence, "From Mexico to California!" I did a double take as I realized that he thought of the transport of illegal aliens from Mexico into California as an underground railroad. I located a large wall map of the United States and traced a highway from just south of the Mexican border to Fresno and talked about the modern-day "underground railroad" that illegal aliens often travel as they come north to the Central Valley to earn money doing agricultural work. Then I pointed out the southern states where slaves lived prior

97

to the Civil War and explained how some slaves traveled north to Ohio and on to Canada while others traveled north through Maryland to Pennsylvania, New York, and New England.

I was amazed by Juan's misunderstanding and his comparison of the slaves to modern-day illegal aliens, and I noticed that most of the Hispanic students had made the same connection. I decided to exploit that connection, and we talked more about the reasons why Mexicans come to our area today and about the dangers they face.

In all, we spent 45 minutes talking about the Underground Railroad and listing words on the chalkboard. Here is their complete list:

Underground Railroad	Quakers
slaves	safe houses
freedom	secret
Harriet Tubman	hide
conductor	wagons, boats, cars
Big Dipper	wanted posters
walked at night	INS agents
not a real railroad	borders
today—Mexico to California	dangers
in 1850—the South to Canada	escape routes
African Americans	hiding places—stations
Mexicans	runaways
scared	19 trips
desperate	saved 300 people
slave states	freed slave
free states	nickname—Moses

DAY 2: WRITING THE TOPIC SENTENCE

The students' teacher kept the word list on the chalkboard and when I arrived the next day, we began by rereading the list. The students remembered the words they had suggested, but I had to remind them about several of the words I had added. This step emphasized to me the importance of ownership: They remembered their own words; I remembered mine. I thought that some of my words—such as *desperate*—were important, so I talked some more about them.

Next I introduced interactive writing, explained how it worked, and passed out extra-large white boards (12 × 18 inches), pens, and sock erasers. I had worried that these 13- and 14-year-old students might find the idea of writing on white boards childish, but they did not. They were eager to begin!

I explained that we were going to write a paragraph on chart paper that we could all read about the Underground Railroad, and that we had to pick an important idea to write about. It had to be something really important, not just a detail. Graciela suggested that we write about the Underground Railroad here in California. I encouraged her idea and suggested that we compare today's "underground railroad" with the earlier one. The group agreed. I also explained that the students would write each sentence on their individual white boards as we wrote on the chart paper.

Our paragraph would have three parts: a topic sentence to introduce the comparison, three comparisons, and a summary sentence. Together we crafted this topic sentence: *The Underground Railroad that slaves traveled to freedom on is like the way Mexicans come to California today to find work.* After we composed the sentence orally, we repeated it several times so everyone could remember it. I heard my sentence structure in the sentence, but all seven students could remember the words and thought of the sentence as theirs. Then we counted the words—our sentence had 21 words!

I asked students to take turns round-robin style coming up to write words on the chart paper taped to the chalkboard. Each student would write one word unless the word was very short, and then he or she would write two words. Armando was first to come up and write. I reminded him to indent before beginning to write and checked that the students indented on their white boards. He wrote *The* and hesitated before writing *Underground*. I encouraged him to check the word wall for the spelling of the word, but Armando acted as though I'd asked him to cheat. I pointed to the word *Underground* on the word wall to encourage him. He asked me if it was all right to copy the word. I encouraged him and the other students to check the word wall anytime they were unsure how to spell a word.

Next Mai came to the chart paper and wrote *Railroad*. Then Juan wrote *That Slaves*, capitalizing both words. I asked him why he capitalized the two words and he explained, "It's what you do when you write. I always start my words with capital letters." Two of the other students agreed with him, and someone pointed out a slogan on the classroom wall on which every word began with a capital letter. I explained that only the most important words—names of people and places—are capitalized. Juan's confusion about capitalizing words illustrates the usefulness of interactive writing. This misconception, along with several others, might never have been clarified if we hadn't been doing an interactive writing activity.

The students continued taking turns writing words, and I used white correction tape to help them correct errors. Several times I asked students to stop writing and to show me their white boards so that I could monitor their writing. Finally, Hua wrote the final word, *work*, and the topic sentence was complete. We reread the sentence several times, and I collected the white boards to hold them until we continued the next day. Because the writing on white boards smudges easily, I was careful not to rub the boards together.

DAYS 3 AND 4: WRITING THE COMPARISONS

On the third day, we began by rereading our first sentence and talking about comparisons between the slaves of the 1850s and the illegal aliens coming from Mexico today. The students mentioned these comparisons, and I made a list on the chalkboard:

The trips are dangerous.

Police hunt for the people who are traveling.

People travel to the north.

There are conductors.

People travel at night.

There are hiding places and safe houses.

They cross rivers and borders.

It took the entire period to compose this list, so on the fourth day, we used some of the comparisons to write the middle section of the paragraph. Using interactive writing, the students wrote these three comparisons: *Both underground railroads are dangerous trips, and they go from south to north. People travel at night and there are hiding places and safe houses on both underground railroads. Just like the slave owners hunted for the escaped slaves, the* INS *agents try to catch the illegal aliens.*

I would have liked to address some contrasts between the slaves and the illegal aliens, but the students recognized few, if any, contrasts, and we were running out of time to complete this project. The students had already written 69 words, their white boards were getting full, and they felt as though they had completed a mammoth task.

DAY 5: WRITING THE CONCLUSION

We wrote the concluding sentence on the fifth day. I began by asking the students to reread what we had written together. Then we picked out the topic sentence, and Ernesto read it aloud. Then we picked out each of the comparisons, and individual students read each one aloud.

Our conclusion was a happy accident: As I was trying to decide how to explain summarizing or drawing a conclusion, Graciela remarked, "We could say that these underground railroads are not underground and they are not railroads." I took advantage of her comment and helped the group expand the sentence to explain why people would risk such danger to travel on an underground railroad. Our concluding sentence was: *When people are desperate they will travel on secret underground railroads that are not underground and are not railroads at all.* Students in the group took turns writing the words on the chart paper, and I noticed that they comfortably used the word wall to check the spelling of some words. Also, Juan was consistently writing words using lowercase letters.

Over 5 days, the students wrote five sentences using conventional spelling and other mechanical skills that demonstrated their understanding of the Underground Railroad. It was an accomplishment that amazed and delighted the students and their teacher. Here is their completed paragraph:

> The Underground Railroad that slaves traveled to freedom on is like the way Mexicans come to California today to find work. Both underground railroads are dangerous trips, and they go from south to north. People travel at night and there are hiding places and safe houses on both underground railroads. Just like the slave owners hunted for the escaped slaves, the INS agents try to catch the illegal aliens. When people are desperate they will travel on secret underground railroads that are not underground and are not railroads at all.

After we reread the paragraph one final time, I word processed it on a computer in the classroom and printed out copies for each of the group members. We decided to leave the chart hanging in the classroom and read the chart aloud to the rest of the class when they returned from the media center. The students were so impressed with their classmates' paragraph that they asked for copies. This group of seven English language learners proudly made copies of their paragraph to share with their classmates.

CONCLUSION

My interactive writing experience with the group of seven eighth graders was successful for several reasons. We connected writing with content-area learning, and through the writing activity, the students clarified and extended their content-area knowledge. They practiced skills in the context of an authentic writing activity, and I had opportunities to model writing strategies, correct misunderstandings, and review spelling, capitalization, and punctuation rules. I also reviewed letter formation and other handwriting skills. The small group size was another factor: I was able to address individual needs, answer questions, and provide more immediate feedback in the small-group setting than I could have with a larger group.

As teachers of older novice writers consider implementing interactive writing, they should remember these guidelines:

- Connect interactive writing to social studies, science, or other content-area study.
- Work in small groups with students at similar developmental levels.
- Use larger white boards so that students have space to write longer sentences and paragraphs.
- Organize sentences into paragraphs.
- Work to craft sophisticated sentences that include key vocabulary words.
- Have students write one or two words rather than single letters when they come up to write on the class chart.

THE MISSING PIECE OF THE PUZZLE

Adrienne L. Herrell

As I enter Mrs. Collom's kindergarten classroom, I look around at the samples of writing displayed on every wall. On one wall are self-portraits the children have drawn; each portrait is labeled with a simple sentence that Mrs. Collom and the child have written interactively. Xiong's says, "Xiong likes ice cream." Maria's says, "Maria likes cats." The writing is wobbly but the words are spelled and spaced correctly.

On another wall is a wall story the children have written as a small-group activity. After reading and singing *Mary Wore Her Red Dress*, the children try on clothing of different colors and compose new verses for the song. The wall story they write interactively contains verses such as "Tia wore her purple sweater" and "Cha wore her pink sunglasses." The verses are written on individual pages of construction paper, illustrated by the child and arranged sequentially to form a wall story.

A chart stand at the front of the room holds yet another interactive writing project. The children write the plan for the day each morning as a whole-group activity. Today's plan says, "Today is Monday. We will paint pictures and write about them." Some children have contributed one letter to the interactive writing chart; others are now able to write a whole word such as *is* or *we*. Soon some children will be able to write a whole sentence interactively, with Mrs. Collom supplying the nonphonetic parts.

The children are writing every day now. It is the second week of October, the sixth week of school. The children in this classroom are all learning English as a second language and are learning to write the same words they are learning to speak. Mrs. Collom uses an alphabet chart, with key pictures for each letter, as she supports their attempts at writing and spelling. She connects the writing to a hands-on experience in which the children have participated. But most important of all, she supports their beginning attempts at composition using interactive writing.

In my capacity as university professor and student teaching supervisor, I spend a lot of time in kindergarten and primary classrooms. I have watched new teaching strategies come and go over a period of almost 40 years. What has happened in classrooms in the past few years as the use of interactive writing has spread from teacher to teacher and from school to school has the power of a revolution in early literacy instruction. Children are learning to use conventional spelling, punctuation, and capitalization. The looks on their faces as they contribute to a class story or write captions for their pictures tell the tale: The children feel powerful as they learn to use their growing knowledge of phonics and spelling patterns. They go back to their journals and self-initiated writing with new vigor. They are learning to write, to spell, to punctuate, and to capitalize. They still use invented spelling in their personal writing but they are incorporating more and more conventional spelling daily. The daily participation in interactive writing is slowly supporting their confidence in themselves as writers and helping them learn the rules of spelling and mechanics.

Some of the classrooms I visit have been used for student teaching over a period of years, so I have been able to witness the change in the children's writing and spelling abilities with the addition of daily interactive writing. Classrooms where children were speaking very little English at the beginning of the year and were barely able to write more than random letters by the end of kindergarten have changed; now, most of the children in these same classrooms, with the same teachers, are able to write entire sentences by the end of the year. Because the teacher and students constantly reread the words that are being written, these same children are also gaining a large sight word vocabulary.

I see the teachers begin the school year with interactive writing. In the first stages, they write just a word or phrase interactively. The length of the interactive writing experience increases daily for the first few months, until an entire story, letter, poem, or description is written each day. The children's knowledge of sight words and sound-symbol relationships seems to grow daily. The evidence of the growth that is most visible is the children's use of conventional spellings and mechanics in their journals and writing center products.

As a result of interactive writing lessons, teachers have daily samples of each child's growing knowledge of phonics, spelling, and writing mechanics. They know which child can write just a letter or two and which child can handle a whole word or sentence. Teachers who use interactive writing also seem to be especially adept at providing just the right amount of support to each child so that everyone feels successful. The fact that children correct their own errors in interactive writing is also a powerful teaching tool. The discussion of the reasons for the use of capital letters, punctuation, and specific spelling patterns provides explicit teaching opportunities with a vital connection to real, meaningful text.

This book is a celebration of interactive writing. The teachers who have written the chapters have all found exciting, innovative ways to harness the power of this effective teaching strategy. They explain the steps in their approach to interactive writing and they share the "missing piece of the puzzle"—the scaffolding of writing with young children. The support and empowerment provided with the use of this technique are obvious. All I need to convince me of the effectiveness of this tool is the faces of the children as they go to the interactive writing chart and write their contribution to the story. The grins that follow their successful writing are the evidence of power. They KNOW they can write.

ABOUT THE AUTHORS

Marlis Becker is a first-grade teacher at Ann Leavenworth Elementary, Center for Accelerated Learning, in Fresno, CA. She has taught since 1989, the majority of the time in primary classes teaching English language learners. She is a Teacher Consultant with the San Joaquin Valley Writing Project.

Linda Boroski is a Teacher on Special Assignment for the Fresno Unified School District as a Miller Unruh Reading Specialist. Her Master's thesis was presented at the California State University Student Research Competition, where it placed first. She is a member of the advisory board for the San Joaquin Valley Writing Project.

Andra Christenson is a kindergarten teacher and primary-grade literacy coach at Wishon Elementary in Fresno, CA. She has developed science education programs for young children and is a Teacher Consultant for the San Joaquin Valley Writing Project.

Kimberly Clark is a curriculum resource teacher and former first-grade teacher at Aynesworth Elementary in Fresno, CA, and has completed her Master of Arts in Reading and Reading Specialist Credential. She is a Teacher Consultant with the San Joaquin Valley Writing Project.

Stephanie Collom is a former kindergarten teacher and is currently a Teacher on Special Assignment in the Fresno Unified School District. She received a Master of Arts in Curriculum and Instruction from California State University, Fresno, and is certified as an Early Childhood Generalist by the National Board of Professional Teaching Standards. She is a Teacher Consultant with the San Joaquin Valley Writing Project.

Michelle Crippen is a former second-grade teacher at Miramonte Elementary in Clovis, CA and currently teaches third grade in Manteca, CA. She has a Master of Arts in Reading and is a Teacher Consultant with the San Joaquin Valley Writing Project.

Adrienne Herrell is a professor of Reading/Language Arts at California State University, Fresno, where she teaches courses in teaching reading to young children. She has also authored books on best practices for second language learners and vocabulary instruction.

Theresa Kasner is a Library Media Teacher at Edison High School in the Fresno Unified School District and is working on her Master's Degree in Library Science. She holds a Master's Degree in Education and a Reading Specialist Credential. She is also a former kindergarten teacher for Sierra Elementary in Tollhouse, CA, where she was teacher of the year. Theresa is a Teacher Consultant with the San Joaquin Valley Writing Project.

Diane Leonard is a first- and second-grade teacher at Balderas Elementary in Fresno, CA. She received a Master of Arts in Curriculum and Instruction from California State University, Fresno. She is a teacher Consultant with the San Joaquin Valley Writing Project.

Susan McCloskey is a first-grade teacher at Greenberg Elementary in Fresno, CA. She is a Master Teacher for California State University, Fresno. Susan has taught classes and workshops focusing on best practices in language arts and is a Teacher Consultant with the San Joaquin Valley Writing Project.

Cynthia Schaefer is a primary teacher at Kirk Elementary in Fresno, CA. She has taught since 1989 in kindergarten through third grade and is a Teacher Consultant with the San Joaquin Valley Writing Project.

Carolyn Stewart is a teacher at Malaga Elementary in Fresno, CA. She is a former kindergarten teacher and currently teaches first and second grades. She has been teaching since 1989 and is a Teacher Consultant with the San Joaquin Valley Writing Project.

Gail Tompkins is a professor of Reading/Language Arts at California State University, Fresno, where she teaches courses in language arts and reading methods. She is director of the San Joaquin Valley Writing Project.